CONSCIOUSLY *Wealthy*

Developing a Rich Mind to Make Power Moves

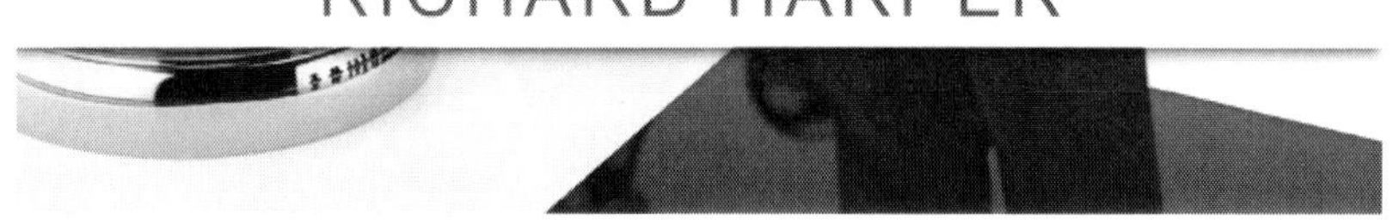

RICHARD HARPER

Consciously Wealthy

Developing a Rich Mind to Make Power Moves

Richard R Harper

Consciously Wealthy
Developing A Rich Mind To Make Power Moves
By Richard R Harper

Published by
Rich Living Media
Printed in the USA.

For bookings or orders
Richard Harper Ministries
P.O. Box 940932
Houston, TX 77079
Phone 832-598-7522
www.richardharperministries.org

Editor: My Best Seller Publishing
Cover Design: MeShayle Lester
Image of chess board with golden pieces © Copyright Tomislav Zivkovic used under license from 123RF
Author Photo: Sabbath Obot
Hairstylist: Bishop Donald E. Williams a.k.a Bishop The Barber

ISBN: 10:0615941168
ISBN-13:978-0615941165

All Scriptures taken from King James Version unless otherwise indicated.

DEDICATION

I dedicate this book to my son Carrington. Daddy wants you to always know that you can *Have*, *Be*, and *Do* whatever you put your mind to. Son, the sky is not your limit in life.

ACKNOWLEDGEMENTS

First, thank you to my heavenly Father for sending His Holy Spirit to whisper this book into my ears.

I would like to acknowledge a group of noble individuals that were God's hands, eyes, and mouth in my life over the years. Without the support of the following people I do not believe that I would have written this book today.

My darling wife Brittney, thank you for sharing me with the world as I developed and wrote this book. Your unfailing love and support has carried me through transitions. I wouldn't have learned a few of these lessons, if you hadn't challenged me five years ago to practice what I preached

My "Eunice and Lois" my mother Linda Brown and grandmother Doris Birch. God truly blessed me when he placed me in both of your care. Before, I knew what a prophet, life coach, or teacher was, you two have been those to me and more.

My spiritual parents Apostle Donald and Prophetess Frances Cleveland. You have lovingly shared your support, prophetic insight, and wisdom with me over the years. Thank you for pushing me.

Dr. Nasir Siddiki, you have not only been a spiritual father but my teacher in understanding the Kingdom of God. Thank you for taking me under your wings as a mentee.

Dr. Shirley K. Clark, you invited me to conduct a workshop during your conference that birthed Consciously Wealthy into a book. Thank you for all of your support over the years.

ACKNOWLEDGEMENTS CONTINUED

Prophet Meshayle Lester, words cannot express how much you and Pastor Don mean to our family. You began as a student but you became a very dear friend and colleague. Thank you for everything that you have done in support of our ministry and this book.

When the student is ready God will send a teacher. Thank you to my wealth and faith teachers that shared with me during different phases of my life: Bishop Larry, Pastor James Harris Sr., Pastor Michael Clerkley, Sr., Pastor Charles Faultry,
Mr. Ron Price, Dr. Mollie Johnson Williams, Linda Splatt,, Sunshine Stanford, Trent and Sara "Diva" Daniel, Bridgette Burns, and Ladymemeh.

I thank my dear friends and family who have been constant source of prayer and encouragement: Hannah's Sons and Daughters International Prayer Ministry, Lighthouse COGIC, Paul Quinn College, Pastor Valentina Shakoni, Prophetess Ada Conner, Dr. Michael Mosely, Zamika Whitfield, Evangelist Linda Goffney, Evangelist Vera Burns, Mrs. Annie Henry, and Ben Harris, Jr.

Thank you, Prevailing Life Kingdom Center for being a supportive church. You all are the greatest congregation in the world

In memory of Mrs. Wiley Harper, Mr. Henry L. Birch, Mother Queen Esther Jones, and Rev William "Bill" Tolbert

I am so very thankful to God for the many voices who have divinely spoke into my life God's greater plan for me. Thank you, to the secret intercessors that have consistently prayed for me when I didn't know it. Thank you, to all of my faithful supporters over the years.

TABLE OF CONTENTS

FOREWORD

Jeremiah 29:11 For I know the thoughts and plans that I have for you, says the Lord, thoughts and plans for welfare and peace and not for evil, to give you hope in your final outcome. God has a good plan for you, a plan to prosper you not to harm you. III John 2 Beloved, I pray that you may prosper in every way and [that your body] may keep well, even as [I know] your soul keeps well and prospers.

The condition to Gius' (In III John 2) prosperity in all things began with prospering his soul - sukea (Greek), mind, will, intellect and emotion. All your wealth begins the same way. As you study the principles in Richard Harper's book, Consciously Wealthy, and apply them you will first change your mindset then the rest of your life.

Study and show yourself approved.

Dr Nasir Siddiki
www.wisdomministries.org

INTRODUCTION

Do you know the laws of the universe? Can you use them to regulate the earth?
Job 38:33 NLT

SUCCESS IS FROM WITHIN

The rules of the game of life are never constant. They change as life progresses. Each phase of life comes with its own set of conventions that govern the outcome. Rules that apply to child's play are obsolete in adult affairs. In my opinion, life's game presents two opportunities; either you are a pawn or a master player. In layman's terms, a pawn is defined as a person or entity used to further the purposes of another. However, a master player is one who is aware of the game change and strategically plays it to win. The purpose of this book is to share with you how to execute the spiritual laws of God to win in your life. God questions Job in Job 38:33, "Do you know the laws of the universe? Can you use them to regulate the earth?" A master player in life will set himself up to understand the spiritual laws of God to create the life he desires to live.

Our educational experiences have for the most part, taught us to look outward to answer questions and solve problems. We generally focus totally on external mediums for success. In our modern information age, it is common practice to begin our search for answers within search engines on the World Wide Web. Most of modern society is so driven by the information highway that the search engine Google, has become a verb instead of a noun. Providing that you are an internet user how many times a day do you automatically search Google for solutions to problems? You may not even realize that the external search engine has become your source for answers.

I believe this reality has created a huge problem for most of our success in life. The issue is not the use of technology or education. The issue is we are losing our abilities to receive solutions for problems from within. I believe God intended for us to manifest success from within instead of without. Our creative edges are becoming dull because we look to what we can see at the end of our fingertips. We no longer pay attention to the still small voice that is speaking on the inside. The still small voice from within is your inner genius.

Some may call this voice intuition, conscious, the prophetic, the Holy Spirit, or even the voice of God. I prefer to call it God's voice. God is speaking but do you really know how to hear Him? They have learned to listen to the inner guide within to make major decisions for their lives, businesses, and ministries. One of the purposes of this book is to teach you how to listen to the voice of Spirit.

Every child is born a genius but their genius is often overshadowed by societal expectations. Each person gifted from God expresses their genius in one particular area or another such as art, athletics, politics, or science. I have met people born with learning or physical disabilities who have accomplished great feats in life. They succeeded because they tapped into a power realm from within. The external world had already counted them out. Therefore their only resource was the power within themselves.

God has no respect of person, Job 34:19 says, "[God] who shows no partiality to princes and does not favor the rich over the poor, for they are all the work of his hands?" One day my mentor, Global Wealth Coach Ladymemeh, said to me, "God doesn't love Mark Zuckerburg, Carlos Slim Helu, Oprah Winfrey, or President Barack Obama any more than He loves you." Her statement immediately bought to my mind Matthew 5:45 that God rains on the just and unjust the same. Ladymemeh went on to say, "It's not a matter of whom God loves the most but it is who you listen to." Ask yourself who you listen to and wait to hear an answer. Who is speaks into your life or spirit constantly? If you listen to idiots (a foolish or stupid person according to Merriam Webster) you will produce idiotic results. Secondly, ask yourself what are you doing with the information you received? Are you applying these principles in your life, business, or ministry, daily? Most of us have heard great principles that we've never actively applied in our lives. Yes, I want to shock your brain a little bit so that you will become conscious concerning where you are at this very moment in your life.

A good friend told me once, "Richard, you have to look at what people do to understand why they are where they are." As you progress in this book, I want you to consciously wake up and observe what you have been doing with your life. I want you to understand why you are not "becoming" who God has designed you to be. The universe and all of the creations of God are ever expanding. My question is why aren't you expanding at this moment? Unfortunately, you will never become, meaning reaching your fullest potential, until you tap into

> "Neither shall they say, Lo here! or, lo there! for, behold, the kingdom of God is within you"
>
> -Luke 17:20

the divine nature of God within yourself. So many people talk about being and that is great because you must first be. However, being is a stand still state; it is not a progressive state. We are becoming our destiny which is a state of progression. Even the universe is expanding at the awesome rate of 46 miles per second. Our spirits are similar to the universe and expand daily. Spiritual expansion is necessary in order to increase your productivity. This means you must expand the capacity of your mind to receive "as a man thinks so is he." You and I are created in the very image of God; this would suggest that everything that is within God is within us. Let me shock you really good now: There was no more God in Jesus than there is in you right now. Of course at this moment I know I have lost the religious and closed-minded people.

However, if you are ready to increase your productivity in life you will read further. In Luke 17:21, Jesus Christ Himself says, "for, behold, the kingdom of God is within you." Which means the same presence of God that was in Jesus is also within you to fulfill your destiny. Furthermore, Romans 8:11 enlightens us more on this concept, "And if the Spirit of him who raised Jesus from the dead is living in you, he who raised Christ from the dead will also give life to your mortal bodies because of his Spirit who lives in you." Hold on friend, don't get any crazy ideas and nail yourself to a cross because the grace of God's kingdom is for you to accomplish your destiny. The world doesn't need a savior because Christ has fulfilled that need. What the world needs to see is men and women of God in the marketplace who operate in the fullness of God's power.

You were not meant only a church member but a citizen of God's kingdom. God's kingdom is so great that we are in it while it is in us. This is a spiritual principle your flesh will never comprehend. As a citizen of God's kingdom you have the power to create the world you want to live in. If you do not like the present world you personally live in financially, relationally, or physically, then you must accept the responsibility that you created it. Being in the kingdom of God has empowered you through both thought and spoken word to create the world you want to live within. God was never concerned with you changing your life; he empowered you to create your world. You must begin to think and act like a king and not a commoner. In the words of my spiritual mentor Dr. Nasir Siddiki, "Kings don't pursue things; things pursue kings, because kings pursue nations." Get into the frame of mind of daily pursuing nations. Think globally every day! A global business, global ministry, global travel, and a global lifestyle are what you want to pursue as a king.

Power Affirmation:

I AM THE CREATOR, THAT THINKS THE THOUGHT THAT CREATES MY WORLD.

So back to the idea of divine nature, you must open your mind and life to the Spirit of God. Continually disregarding the word of God and the purpose of God for your life will hinder you from fully operating in the Spirit. Heaven will become a brass ceiling for you until you acknowledge the presence of heaven in your life. Furthermore, heaven will never move for Earth until Earth makes the first move. Many people say they hear the voice of God. I beg to differ because you will never hear His voice without His presence. You need to have an open heaven in your life to receive divine intelligence. In this book I will lay out for you my step-by-step biblical process to keep heaven opened in your life. Heaven has blessings so large for you that you will never be able to contain them. Heaven's blessings are generational. The journey you are embarking upon will change things in major ways for generations to come, even after you have passed on. Don't get overwhelmed. I will explain these concepts more throughout the book.

CHAPTER ONE

I have said, Ye are gods; and all of you are children of the most High.
Psalm 82:6

ACKNOWLEDGE YOUR DIVINE NATURE

Your very being is divine, according to the Bible. In 1 Thessalonians 5:23, you are first, spirit; next, soul (mind); and finally body. Let's explore the concepts of divine nature so that you will better understand the untapped power reservoir within. Man is created in the image and likeness of God and He breathed His spirit into man's body. The breath of God is the Spirit of God. When God blew His breath which is His Spirit into Adam, Adam became a living soul. Notice further that man had absolutely no life devoid of Spirit. If you continue to ignore the divine presence of God in your life you will never experience abundant living. Living comes from the Hebraic word "chai" (pronounced: hay) is defined as lively active, in reference to man. Also, the Hebraic word for soul is "nephesh" (pronounced: neh-fesh) which is defined as seat of mind, desire, emotion, and passion. In a raw definition, we can define living soul as a lively active seat of your mind, desire, emotions, and passions. Therefore, it is Spirit that activates your mind, desires, emotions, and passions. The Holy Spirit brings life into dead situations. According to 2 Corinthians 3:6, "for the letter kills, but the spirit gives life." This leads me to ask again whose voice are you listening to. What Spirit is driving your mind, desires, emotions, and passions? Is it the Spirit of God or a negative spirit that drives you daily?" As you read earlier, "And if the Spirit of Him who raised Jesus from the dead is living in you, He who raised Christ from the dead will also give life to your mortal bodies because of His Spirit who lives in you."

In John 14:2 Jesus said, "In my Father's house are many mansions: if it were not so, I would have told you. I go to prepare a place for you." Most people that have attended church for a length of time usually think of dying and going to heaven when they hear these verses. This is partially true about heaven but why can't we experience heaven on Earth? Jesus said in His Father's house are many mansions. In the scripture God's house is His kingdom, and we are the mansions within His house. God's kingdom is so great that we are in it while it is within us. Our natural minds will never comprehend this possibility but our Spirits will agree that it is truth. You are a mansion located in the kingdom of God. Mansions are very expensive homes that are carefully constructed with only the finest of material owned exclusively by the wealthy and elite. If a mansion is given to someone who doesn't realize its value, they will treat it as a common shack. Your life is

> In my Father's house are many mansions: if it were not so, I would have told you. I go to prepare a place for you.
>
> – John 14:2

invaluable and must be carefully constructed with only the finest of material. Ask yourself this question: Am I living in a mansion with a shack mentality? The Bible declares we are the physical temples of God and His Spirit dwells within us, therefore it is most apropos that He would dwell in an exquisite home. In the Old Testament, the Ark of the Covenant was the physical sign of the presence of God; therefore, He gave detailed instructions on how it should be constructed. He demanded that it be crafted with the finest material. The Ark of the Covenant doesn't represent the dwelling place of God anymore but you and I do. Jesus also told His disciples in John 14 that He was going to prepare a place for them so that where He was going they could also be. Jesus accomplished this by shedding His blood on the cross at Calvary. The blood of Jesus prepares us to be the perfect dwelling place for the presence of God. If you are not a follower of Christ, I encourage you to keep reading. I am not here to beat you over the head with salvation. However, I do want you to see why I believe that Jesus Christ is the door to living in oneness with God. You might have read what other spiritual philosophers have to say about your success and purpose in life, so please do not close your mind to this book. I am here to help you experience a better life, not to condemn you.

We were placed on Earth to operate as God in the earth realm. I like what Dr. Bill Winston says in his book *The Kingdom of God in You*, "God created humans in His image and in His class, as under-rulers in the earth. Humans didn't create God. The created will never be God. We will never be El Shaddai, God Almighty, yet God gave us authority and responsibility over the earth's resources."(Winston, 2006)

Genesis 1:26-28 AMP

26 God said, Let Us [Father, Son, and Holy Spirit] make mankind in Our image, after Our likeness, and let them have complete authority over the fish of the sea, the

> birds of the air, the [tame] beasts, and over all of the earth, and over everything that creeps upon the earth.
> 27 So God created man in His own image, in the image and likeness of God He created him; male and female He created them.
> 28 And God blessed them and said to them, Be fruitful, multiply, and fill the earth, and subdue it [using all its vast resources in the service of God and man]; and have dominion over the fish of the sea, the birds of the air, and over every living creature that moves upon the earth.

In order to function as God in the earth we must be infused with His Spirit. Without the Spirit of God acting as a liaison, this would absolutely be impossible. God told us in the book of Isaiah that His thoughts were not our thoughts. His thoughts were naturally on a higher plane. However, God didn't say that we could not access His thoughts. God's thoughts are supernaturally transmitted and create supernatural results. Since God desires to communicate with us, He mandated His spirit, which is the Holy Spirit to govern the communication process.

Consequently, without the Holy Spirit we have a major dilemma in communicating with God. Romans 8:26 details our dilemma by saying, "In the same way, the Spirit helps us in our weakness. We do not know what we ought to pray for, but the Spirit himself intercedes for us with groans that words cannot express." We haven't the foggiest idea of what we should be pray for in regards to the abundant plan of God for our lives. 1 Corinthians 2:11 declares, "For who among men knows the thoughts of a man except the man's spirit within him? In the same way no one knows the thoughts of God except the Spirit of God."

Let me illustrate this idea for you. In this scenario we will say that God wants to bless Jane with a brand new car, fully loaded with all the options. However, Jane is praying for a car that will only get her from point A to point B because she is only conscious of her limited resources. God answers Jane's prayer and through His permissive gives her the car that she asked for. However, that car was not God's plan for her.

God has two types of wills, which are called sovereign and permissive will. God's sovereign will means He has the right to do whatever He wants in His good pleasure. God's permissive will means that God allows us to have or do what we want even when it is not the best thing for us.

Over a course of time Jane became dissatisfied with her car because it isn't very reliable. So she begins to think about getting rid of the car, this time she allows the Holy Spirit to lead her in praying for her next car.

When you allow the Holy Spirit to lead you in prayer you may receive a vision, thought, or speak in an unknown tongue coupled with a feeling of peace concerning the will of God. The Holy Spirit knows God wants you to have a brand new car with all of the options and leads you to pray for this type of car. God happily initiates through the universe events and opportunities for you to have this car.

Had Jane allowed the Holy Spirit to facilitate the spiritual dialogue between her and God, she would have been driving the brand new car all along. In addition, God provided an increase in her income that would pay for the car.

The initial self-led prayer even caused a delay financial increase. This occurs because we naturally cannot speak or interpret God's supernatural language.

> You must be properly aligned subconsciously with the super conscious which is your divine mind.

Right now perhaps God is speaking to you in visions, inspirations, or desires to have greater than what you have presently. Those inspirations often nudge you at different times, nudging you concerning what you should *be*, *do*, and *have*. You may drive by neighborhoods that you should be living in; or pass a university you should have attended; ignore careers or things you should be doing. Remaining unconscious of these God visions leaves you perhaps unfulfilled.

This is because your natural mind alone will never accept the infinite possibilities of God as a reality until you are first convinced by the Spirit they are real. One of my foundational Scriptures is 2 Corinthians 2:9-10 which says, "However, as it is written: No eye has seen, no ear has heard, no mind has conceived, what God has prepared for those who love him, but God has revealed it to us by his Spirit. The Spirit searches all things, even the deep things of God." The Spirit of God enables us to be prophetically intelligent to know the higher thoughts of God.

Satan is our adversary and he will do everything in his ability to hinder the advancement of the kingdom of God. The kingdom of God is within you; therefore, Satan has to hinder your success in his efforts to hinder the kingdom of God. Whether you know it or not, your God-ordained destiny will bring redemption to the land. This is why your success is very vital to God's plan for kingdom advancement. God tells us in Deuteronomy 8:18, "But thou shalt remember the Lord thy God: for it is he that giveth thee power to get wealth." Please don't allow any religious people to influence you to believe you cannot please God if you are wealthy. Would you honestly allow yourself to follow the leadership of an impoverished and unstable person? Your effectiveness in ruling and reigning in your world is based upon your consciousness of God's spirit within you.

CHAPTER TWO

Who against hope believed in hope, that he might become the father of many nations, according to that which was spoken, So shall thy seed be
Romans 4:18 KJV

CONSCIOUSLY WEALTHY

The key to your wealth, health and success is your state of consciousness. You may possibly be questioning my use of the word consciousness especially considering that I am a Christian author. Everything organic is created with an atomic structure and each atom has at least a minimal level of consciousness. Your organs have a level of consciousness within your body. When something is wrong in your body, your organs communicate pain, tiredness, hunger, or thirst. Animals have the ability to communicate with each other and humans. If you are a pet owner, take notice of how your pet responds to the thoughts and emotions you transmit. Research has revealed that plants have the ability to respond to thoughts whether they are of positive or negative emotional energy. Scientific studies have proven that minerals have a level of consciousness.

So what is consciousness? A dictionary definition of consciousness is the quality or state of being aware, especially of something within oneself. However, the meaning of consciousness is much deeper; it refers to awareness of self. Consciousness is who we are. God the creator flows through our conscious manifesting things out of our own awareness. Consciousness is the income of your mind. You have purchased what you have in your life with your own conscious awareness.

Consciousness also means to be present in all of the journeys of your life. You must be present in your endeavors in order to be successful in them. Most people go through life without ever being present in their own life. Those people are unmotivated about and live as if they are zombies. They are in a constant cycle of mundaness living devoid of excitement, achievement, or success. Begin to ask yourself now what is the purpose of my life? Am I excited about each day I live? What motivates me to do more? If you can't answer these questions, it's time to realize you are not present in your life

Conscious awareness of self is how we define ourselves. Your definition of self or self-concept, greatly affects your behavior patterns. Your success in life is heavily predicated upon your behavior patterns. There will always be situations that are out of your control but you can control your response to those situations. Murmuring and complaining about tough circumstances will hold you in a place of lower consciousness. You will miss the opportunities or events that can create abundance in your life. Missed opportunities always lead to poverty. Poor stands for *Passing-Over-Opportunities- Repeatedly*. Remember, money is not and will never be evil but it is the love of money that is the root of evil. Everyone must examine their personal motive for wealth and success. Your personal motive for what you want in life will develop your pattern to achieve it.

Consciousness Is Biblical

Yes, dear friend, consciousness is very biblical and this is why you are living with a blurred view of your success in life. Consciousness isn't some new age jargon. The Apostle Peter wrote in 1 Peter 5:8 (MSG), "Keep a cool head. Stay alert. The Devil is poised to pounce, and would like nothing better than to catch you napping. Keep your guard up."In other words, Peter is instructing us to be conscious or aware of the enemy of our mind. Your level of awareness denotes your state of consciousness. Whenever you are not conscious of the moment or the world in which you live, that means you are unconscious. Research shows us that the average person thinks at least 60,000 thoughts per day. Out of 60,000 thoughts per day most people more than likely do not remember at least 97 percent of those thoughts.

Here is proof of your state of unconsciousness. Has anyone ever walked up behind you while watching television, reading, or sitting and that person frightened the daylights out of you? Why did you get so afraid? It's because you were unaware of your environment--unconscious. Had you been paying attention to your surroundings you would have realized that someone was walking up behind you. Here's another example, have you held a conversation with someone and afterward you realized you did not hear a word they said to you? Although, you paid attention to them intently-- you even nodded your head, or gave other signals that you were with them in the conversation, however, if you were offered a million dollars to repeat the conversation, you would have to be a million dollars less because you were not conscious of the moment. What happened? You missed the moment. Think about the time when you were reading a book and you missed an entire page because your mind was somewhere else.

People live in these states of unconsciousness every single day of their lives. Couples are unconscious of their relationships so they miss out on true love. Parents are not conscious of their children's childhood so they miss those important hallmarks of growth. How many worship services have we sat in and not experienced an encounter with a very present God? These are all examples of invaluable losses people suffer every day because they are unconscious. Unconsciousness is fine when you are unconsciously producing positive results. There are people who win without ever trying. You must make successful conscious efforts to produce successful unconscious results.

Three Levels of Consciousness

Consciousness is a highly researched topic in psychology, neuroscience, and other fields that study mind science. There are numerous questions concerning whether or not consciousness exists in non-humans? At what fetal stage do unborn children become conscious? Is it possible to programmed computers with consciousness? Consciousness is the place within where your awareness of self is located. Consciousness is arranged into three areas: conscious, subconscious, and super conscious.

The conscious mind is the state of mind when you are awake or aware; this is what you are using now as you read this book. It is with the conscious mind that you think, reason, and make daily decisions. Your conscious mind analyzes situations and formulates a perception of the situation and relays to the body how you should react to the situation based upon the perception. In addition, the conscious mind chooses what is to be accepted or rejected into your subconscious mind. You can consciously decide what you want to create by accepting or rejecting ideas. It is within your conscious mind that you develop your likes

> You must be properly aligned subconsciously with the super conscious which is your divine mind.

True success is when you are living the plan of God for your life.

and dislikes, perceptions, beliefs, and paradigms. That information is stored in your subconscious mind. It is with your conscious mind that you program your subconscious mind in how you will function during every moment of your life. A computer is controlled by an operating system such as Microsoft Windows, but the operating system is programmed by a programmer who has decided how the computer will function for the user. Your life functions in the same manner and you must become the programmer of your mind. Consciously decide what you will program into your life. You have absolute control over your conscious mind and what you accept as truth.

The subconscious mind is timeless, and works in present tense only. It stores past learning experiences and memories, and it monitors all of your bodily operations, function, heart rate, etc. The subconscious mind is so intricate it has an expanded process capacity enabling it to manage thousands of events at one time. This is why you do not have to think to perform bodily functions.

It thinks literally and will accept every thought your conscious mind chooses to accept. The subconscious mind is similar to the universe in that it does not discern what you consider good or bad, wanted or unwanted. It only stores the data that you consciously accept as reality. Your subconscious mind is very much like a computer; it accepts whatever you program it to perform. Bearing this in mind you should realize that whatever you put "IN" is what will come "OUT." Your subconscious mind is always working hard to create the images you are projecting from your mind. When you reason within your conscious mind that something is fearful, then your subconscious mind causes your body to react in fear. Programming your subconscious for success will result in unconscious successful habits.

Hopefully by now you are becoming aware of the fact that your life is being created by your mental state. It is important that you know that your mind and brain are two different entities. The brain is a physical entity and the mind is a spiritual entity. Spiritual beings express themselves through physical bodies. For example, God is a spirit and He works through human beings to perform certain tasks. When I taught computer classes years ago, I always explained to students that hardware was anything on the computer that you could touch and software was the part that you couldn't touch. Your brain is the hardware and your mind is the software that directs your functions.

Finally, the super conscious is what I prefer to call the mind of God existing in our minds. You may also describe the super conscious as the great I AM. I AM is one of the names of God. The super conscious is like a computer connected to the internet. The internet enables computers to access information and communicates within seconds across the globe. Within the mind of God, lie infinite possibilities with no boundaries or limits.

All things that exist are first conceived within God's mind. The super conscious provides divine intelligence to us that I like to categorize as prophetic intelligence and emotional intelligence. Prophetic intelligence is divine knowledge of what is to come beyond natural knowledge. On the other hand, emotional intelligence is your awareness of how you perceive, react, and control your emotions. These intelligences are communicated to our conscious mind by the super conscious. It is your responsibility to accept or reject the intelligence. God will never force you to believe.

Our minds are infinitesimal when compared to the mind of God. We can learn more about God's mind by considering Isaiah 55:8-9 which says, "For my thoughts are not your thoughts, neither are your ways my ways, saith the Lord. For as the heavens are higher than the earth, so are my ways higher than your ways, and my thoughts than your thoughts." This is why it is necessary that you function on a higher level of consciousness in order to receive the entire good God has available for you.

The Bible makes this point clear in Isaiah 60:1-5, "Arise, shine, for your light has come, and the glory of the Lord rises upon you. See, darkness covers the earth and thick darkness is over the peoples, but the Lord rises upon you and his glory appears over you. Nations will come to your light, and kings to the brightness of your dawn. Lift up your eyes and look about you: All assemble and come to you; your sons come from afar, and your daughters are carried on the hip. Then you will look and be radiant, your heart will throb and swell with joy; the wealth on the seas will be brought to you, to you the riches of the nations will come."

The command of God is for you to arise and shine, in other words, rise to a higher level of consciousness. Why? Because, the presence of God through His spirit has come into your life to bring you divine intelligence. The light is symbolic of divine intelligence which you may refer to as revelation.

The Scripture says lift up your eyes and look around you, which speaks to you raising your mind's eye to a higher spiritual plane so that you can see beyond your present reality. You are surrounded by infinite possibilities of abundance, health, wealth, peace and prosperity. You will not achieve them until you first see them. Remember without realization there is no materialization. When you believe what is available to you within the mind of God, all mental and spiritual blockages will be broken so that you will begin to flow abundantly.

Money flows because it is a current of energy. Think about it. We call money currency because it flows as a current from one stream to the next. I do not want you to get caught up in money. It is important for you to understand that money is not the only manifestation of wealth. There are many people that have money but are consciously poor.

The true wealth of God is intangible. Jesus said the poor will be with you always. There will always be people who are spiritually and naturally poor. God's blessings flow continually from you to others around you. Your heart or subconscious mind will begin to reverence the presence of God in you. Your capacity to receive more will increase because of the abundance that will manifest through events and opportunities in your life. These events and opportunities will supernaturally occur in your life because the forces of the Gentiles, which represent the worldly material, will be at your beckoning call.

Kingdom Consciousness

The higher level of consciousness I am speaking of is what I call kingdom consciousness. Both kingdoms of heaven and earth were first created in the mind of God. Every infinite possibility for you is within the kingdom of God. From the kingdom of God, universal laws are legislated that work either for us or against us each and every day. There are universal laws such as the Law of Sowing and Reaping, Law of Love, or the Law of Vibration just to name a few. All universal laws respond to what we project without regard to whether we wanted it or not. I am going to explain this principle more in depth within the book.

Awareness of the kingdom of God within you is necessary to activate the possibilities for your life. Jesus began his earthly ministry preaching repent for the kingdom of heaven is at hand in Matthew 4:10. In the Greek translation, repent comes from the word "metanoeō,' which means to change your mind for the better. The reality of the kingdom will not manifest until you change the pattern of your thinking.

Consciousness means to be present in all of the journeys of your life.

Kingdom consciousness will cause you to think, speak, and respond differently to life. You will shift from a natural style of living into living in the supernatural. I use the word supernatural because you will experience simple miracles daily. Things that would ordinarily take months or years to happen for others will happen for you in days or weeks because of the supernatural power of God's kingdom. The kingdom way of thinking is a winner's way of thinking.

Conscious Creation

I believe there is a reason why bad things happen to good people. Whether you choose to accept it or not, every human on Earth is contributing to a collective consciousness that is creating good and bad events in the Earth. If we look closely at Matthew 18:19, which incidentally is a powerful Scripture for good, it says, "That if two of you shall agree on earth as touching anything that they shall ask, it shall be done for them of my Father which is in heaven."Jesus didn't necessarily say that the Law of Agreement was only for good things in this verse. People collectively agree with such negative beliefs such as the world is bad, you can't trust people, there aren't any jobs, or it's the next ethnic group's fault, without realizing they are creating these horrible realities for themselves through a lower state of consciousness. For every effect in this world there is a cause and the consciousness of mankind is the cause.

Unfortunately, the super conscious, like the subconscious, does not discriminate between what you want or do not want. You will receive from the super conscious whatever you are projecting into it whether good or bad. I base this belief on Proverbs 23:7, "For as he thinks in his heart, so is he."You will only receive what you put out into the universe. Now I know you are thinking, Richard are you telling me that God will even give me the bad I unintentionally asked for? Yes, I am saying just that. In the

Bible, Job experienced a horrible ordeal. Job, one of the richest men in the bible became gravely ill, lost every single possession he owned, and his children. Most of the times in church, when we talk about Job we mostly refer to him being a great example of not losing faith during a trial. This is very true. Job is a great example of steadfast faith in adversity. However, I always questioned why God allowed Satan to take all of Job's possessions and health. Job 1:7-8 states, "The LORD said to Satan, Where have you come from? Satan answered the LORD, From roaming through the earth and going back and forth in it. Then the LORD said to Satan, Have you considered my servant Job? There is no one on earth like him; he is blameless and upright, a man who fears God and shuns evil.'" You are probably thinking God recommended Job to be tempted of Satan because he had great moral character. Your answer is partially correct. Let me show you another verse in Job's story. Job sheds light on why God was allowed to offer him to Satan for testing in Job 3:25, "What I (Job) *feared* most has come upon me; what I *dreaded* has happened to me." If Job feared this thing the most that means he had a full list of fears. By now I hope you are seeing the pattern, God didn't intend for Job to experience the horrible trial that he faced. Job's subconscious fear created an open opportunity for Satan to release chaos in his life.

Remember that God's Universal Laws do not decipher between wanted and unwanted. The law of sowing and reaping found in Galatians 6:7 says that whatever you sow you will reap. Imagine your mind as a garden and whatever seeds you plant in it will grow. Galatians 6:8 (NLV) says, "The one who sows to please his sinful nature, from that nature will reap destruction; the one who sows to please the Spirit, from the Spirit will reap eternal life."

The super conscious is the ultimate source for prosperity. Therefore, your subconscious mind must be properly aligned with the super conscious (mind of God in you). Here is food for thought. If you can communicate with

God then it is equally possible for God to communicate with you.

Your Subconscious Creates Your Reality

Your subconscious belief system is determining at this very moment the level of success that you will achieve in life. Here is a side bar note for you: Success should never be based upon the size of an individual's bank account, socio - economic status, or material possessions.

You must consciously decide to delete every limiting belief you have embraced in your subconscious mind. God only has good thoughts concerning you according to Jeremiah 29:11, "For I know the thoughts that I think toward you, saith the Lord, thoughts of peace, and not of evil, to give you an expected end." You will never materialize what you have not realized. Becoming conscious of the kingdom of God will reveal the good plans God has thought concerning you. Do you know the good thoughts and plans that God has in mind for you?

Let me give you an example of a young man that was in unnecessary fear, because he was unconscious of God's protective presence in his life. In 2 Kings 2:14-17 NIV, (one of my favorite stories), we read, "Then he sent horses and chariots and a strong force there. They went by night and surrounded the city. When the servant of the man of God got up and went out early the next morning, an army with horses and chariots had surrounded the city. Oh no, my lord! What shall we do? The servant asked. 'Don't be afraid,' the prophet answered. Those who are with us are more than those who are with them.' And Elisha prayed, 'Open his eyes, Lord, so that he may see.' Then the Lord opened the servant's eyes,

> God has great dreams and visions that are stored in the inside of you.

and he looked and saw the hills full of horses and chariots of fire all around Elisha."

Prophet Elisha's servant is a prime example of a person that lives in the lower conscious realm. He had a fear and scarcity mentality. The young man was unconscious of God's provision. Thankfully, Elisha operated on a higher plane of consciousness and had no fear of the enemy. Elisha prayed that the young man's eyes would be opened to see who was really with him. Miraculously, he saw horses and chariots of fire in the hills surrounding Elisha. Notice the horses and chariots of fire were positioned in the hills above the enemy. God had already provided the protection for Elisha against his enemies. So Elisha had no need to fear.

Ask yourself what things are your presently fearing? At this moment what are you most fearful of? You are afraid because you do not realize the God's plan of provision. You may be presently fearful of debt, illness, the lack of relationship, foreclosure, unemployment, or even success at this very moment. Job, in his subconscious mind projected an image of fear that created events to validate his fear.

Personally, I do not care to give the devil anymore mention than he should receive. However, I believe he does exist. Denying his existence doesn't make him any less active. One definition I give the devil is anything that attacks the productivity of your mind resulting in your being unsuccessful in life. The Bible says give no place to the devil, (Ephesians 4:27). In other words, you must stop providing accommodations in your mind to those things that attack it. Please ask yourself this question, does it make any sense for me to sleep with my enemy at night? Affirm this now and Keep saying it until you get excited about it.

MY MIND IS NO LONGER A HOTEL FOR THE DEVIL! I ONLY ALLOW THOUGHTS IN MY MIND THAT SUPPORT THE ABUNDANT PLAN OF GOD FOR ME!

CHAPTER THREE

For as he thinketh in his heart, so is he...
Proverbs 23:7

PROPHETIC INTELLIGENCE

The Spirit of God is a creative life-giving force. Genesis 1:1-2 (AMP) "In the beginning God (prepared, formed, fashioned, and) created the heavens and the earth. The earth was without form and an empty waste, and darkness was upon the face of the very great deep. The Spirit of God was moving (hovering, brooding) over the face of the waters."

As God was creating the heavens and the earth through the spoken word, the Holy Spirit began to move giving life to what was spoken. Remember you have the same creative power to speak and manifest your desires in your world. One of the keys to your success as a conscious creator is prophetic intelligence. Prophetic Intelligence is a spiritual knowledge that is gained only through divine revelation. The divine nature of God within you is a prophetic nature. You have the power to manifest your metaphysical vision into a physical reality. Wow!

It is imperative that you be observant of what you are speaking. Your words are simultaneously creating your reality. Your entire world is framed by the powerful words that you are releasing.

The Holy Spirit provides us with spiritual revelation that surpasses all natural information we can learn. Look at John 16:16, "Howbeit when he, the Spirit of truth, is come, he will guide you into all truth: for he shall not speak of himself; but whatsoever he shall hear, that shall he speak: and he will shew you things to come." The Holy Spirit is the Spirit of Truth and one of His mandates is to guide you into all truth.

How many pitfalls would have been avoided if you knew that someone was telling you a lie? The world has taught us that we must learn by trial and error. Of course, this is partially true. The testing of your faith develops patience. Being led by the Holy Spirit helps you avoid entering into trials. Those trials were never intended by God for you to face. We live in a world that loves to glamorize lies. Lies sell and produce major dollars for tabloids and entertainment gossip shows every day. Aren't you ready for the truth to operate in your life?

Secondly, we learn that the Holy Spirit does not speak out of His own authority but He only reports back to you what the Father (God) has spoken to Him. All of God's words are true and will never fail to accomplish their assignment.

Thirdly, the Holy Spirit will show you what is to come, in other words, the future. Isaiah 45:3 says, "I will give you the treasures of darkness, riches stored in secret places, so that you may know that I am the LORD, the God of Israel, who summons you by name." The Holy Spirit reveals God's plan

> You must have a conscious awakening to see higher

for your life. Jeremiah 29:11 tells you that God has good thoughts about you and has designed an awesome plan for your life. However, you will never realize the plan of God for your life until you tap into your divine nature. God's thoughts and plans for you are far beyond whatever you could think or ever imagine for yourself.

One of the foundational scriptures in this book is Isaiah 55:8-9, "For my thoughts are not your thoughts, neither are your ways my ways, saith the Lord. For as the heavens are higher than the earth, so are my ways higher than your ways, and my thoughts than your thoughts." We've established the fact that God transmits His thoughts at a higher level of frequency than we naturally do. The good news is that the Spirit of God within enables you to receive the thoughts being transmitted from God into your conscious mind.

Elevation to a higher level of consciousness is how you comprehend the divine intelligence from God. Here is an example that better explains this concept. When you're in your car driving and have the radio on, you may be listening to your favorite broadcast on the AM station. However, as you travel a few miles down the road you might find yourself out of the range of the radio station's signal although you are still in the same city. You may decide to switch to an FM station which has a much higher frequency than AM. However, as you travel a bit further you realize that the station number is still the same but the broadcast content has changed. Perhaps you were listening to cool jazz but now the content is country and western. You get fed up and subscribe to a satellite radio service

> For I know the thoughts that I think toward you, saith the Lord, thoughts of peace, and not of evil, to give you an expected end.
>
> ~Jeremiah 29:11

> You become wealthy today by solving today's problems.

that will allow you to listen to the same broadcast throughout your journey uninterrupted.

To hear the satellite programming you must upgrade your equipment and pay the subscription cost. Are you willing to invest in an upgrade for your life?

How do you see yourself in light of this example? You may be on an AM frequency and whatever insights you received from God faded away with distance. Perhaps you are little more enthused and you're on an FM frequency but as you progressed you lost focus. You sporadically shift from one project to another without ever completing one. My hope is that you are like one of those satellite radio subscribers. You are completely focused on your goals and willing to upgrade to a higher frequency.

The only difference between a successful person and an unsuccessful person is that the successful person got out of bed and did what the unsuccessful person wouldn't do. The successful person wants to sleep in late, enjoy entertainment, date and have fun. Yet, the successful person realizes they will not achieve success if they do not discipline themselves to create the life that they want to live. Even Jesus Himself said, "I must work the works of him that sent me, while it is day: the night cometh, when no man can work." You only have today to seize but it will pass you by if you do not tap into your divine nature.

Two of my favorite Scriptures, which are foundational for most of my teachings, are 1 Corinthians 2:9 and 10. 1 Corinthians 2:9-10 states, "However, as it is written: What no eye has seen, what no ear has heard, and what no human mind has conceived the things God has prepared for those who love him these are the things God has revealed to us by his Spirit" Your natural eyes, ears, and human mind will never fathom the things that God has in store for you. They are only revealed to you through prophetic intelligence by the Spirit of God. Please don't rejoice now because you will miss the best part of the text. In verses 11 and 12 we read, "For who knows a person's thoughts except their own spirit within them? In the same way no one knows the thoughts of God except the Spirit of God. What we have received is not the spirit of the world, but the Spirit who is from God, so that we may understand what God has freely given us." Man will never be able to explain the mysteries of God through natural understanding. Only the Spirit of God can reveal to man the things of God. The best part is the Spirit of God will show you all of the things that are freely given to you. Now think to yourself, what have I paid too much for in my life? God has given you all things that pertain to life and godliness. God also has given you all things richly to enjoy. You can release your faith for these categories.

Unfortunately, you are paying too much for what God has already purchased. Until now you may have been out of touch with your divine nature. As Jesus was teaching His disciples about the Holy Spirit He explained in John 16:15, "All that belongs to the Father is mine. That is why I said the Spirit will receive from me what he will make known to you." Jesus wanted us to understand that everything that belong to God also belong to Him. Now because we are in Him, the Holy Spirit would show us where these treasures are and we can use them at any time. Your health, wealth, peace, and prosperity are sitting in front of you, but you are unaware of them.

The Holy Spirit is such a liberating force transcending space and time. Prophetic intelligence empowers you to be limitless in your pursuits of health, wealth, peace, and prosperity. Acts 1:8 tells us that after the Holy Spirit has come upon us we shall receive power. I don't want to focus on the theological sense of power but rather the metaphoric sense of power which is influence.

Prophetic Intelligence enables you to have Oprah influence, Barak Obama influence, but greater God influence. Prophetic intelligence is accurate intelligence and is vital to your being an influential person. People look to be led by accurate leaders who are relevant to the times. Consumers purchase relevant products that will meet today's demands. People only connect with ministries that meet relevant needs in their life.

No one wants to follow, support, or subscribe to anything that is inaccurate. The right word at the wrong time is simply the wrong thing to say, there are no exceptions. I'm saying the right word at the wrong time because every prophetic word has an appropriate time. Very often people have the right idea that was implemented at the wrong time, resulting in failure. Millions of dollars are wasted when an individual had a great product that was introduced to the world at the wrong time.

Moreover, you must develop concepts that will solve the problems of tomorrow. Companies such as Apple or Microsoft have prototypes for technology that are not planned for release for years out, waiting for the right moment to solve a problem. Prophetic intelligence provides you foresight that will allow you to be futuristic in your thinking. Only futuristic thinkers will maximize future once in a lifetime moments. Just imagine how much money you would have today if you would have invested in Facebook, Google, or Starbucks in their infancy. There is a possibility that your business or ministry may be one of those concepts that will be worth billions in the future.

Prophecy is for those that believe according to 1Corinthians 14:22, "Prophecy, however, is for believers, not for unbelievers." You must have belief in God's presence in you to hear or see what He is saying concerning you.

I would like to share a story with you of how Conrad Hilton founder of the Hilton Hotel chain used intuition or what I call prophetic intelligence to make his fortune. It is apparent that Conrad Hilton relied on his prophetic intelligence to make his fortune. Hilton always denied having any prophetic or psychic abilities; however his intuition was so uncanny that even he often amazed himself. "Most of the time I can reconstruct the circumstances of these hunches," he stated, "and I can figure out in a general way where it came from. I mean I can explain it—not completely but enough to make it less strange. There have been times, though, when I couldn't come up with a good explanation."

Once, his remarkable intuition helped him buy a prestigious old hotel in Chicago. The sale was based on sealed bids. All of the bids were to be opened on a select day and the hotel would go to the highest bidder. Some days prior to the deadline, Hilton offered a bid of $165,000, but that night he went to bed feeling restless and did not sleep well. The next morning he changed his mind. "It just didn't feel right," he said afterward. He increased his bid to $180,000. This was just right—he outbid his close rival by a mere $200.

At this point you should desire to shift into a higher frequency for prophetic intelligence. I am certain that your success muscles are being strengthened and you are ready to move into action. This is a good thing; there is more insight to gain.

CHAPTER FOUR

For the kingdom of God is not meat and drink; but righteousness and peace, and joy in the Holy Ghost
Romans 14:17

EMOTIONAL INTELLIGENCE

Our emotions are our internal pointing system locating and guiding us on our journey to destiny. I have been guilty in the past of encouraging people to ignore how they felt in difficult situations. At times, your emotions can trick you out of opportunities if you focus too much on them. However, I was enlightened when I heard the late Reverend Frederick J. Eikerenkoetter II (Rev. Ike) say in a sermon, "Tell your feelings how to feel." There is absolutely nothing wrong with paying attention to how you feel. The principle key is to know why you feel the way you feel. Students of the Law of Attraction understand that you will only manifest what you feel most strongly about. For instance, if you feel negative about rich people it will be very difficult for you to manifest riches. The Holy Spirit reveals to us our emotional state. This is referred to as emotional intelligence. Emotional intelligence is your ability to perceive, control, and analyze your emotions. Many people are emotionally ignorant. Usually they will blame every external factor before turning within to examine their emotional state. Also, emotionally ignorant people are unaware of how they affect others emotionally. Your life is your responsibility, and it flows from your state of consciousness. Emotional intelligence is necessary to pinpoint those defeating emotions you hold subconsciously.

Your conscious mind only passes images to your subconscious mind for storage that you have attached an intense emotion with. For instance, your fear of something or your enjoyment of something is all stored in your subconscious mind. The attachment of intense emotion validates the thought or image. I recall as a child my great grandmother was terribly frightened of snakes. She would hide her face at the sight of a snake on television. Subconsciously she had attached an emotion of fear with the snake. Her fear made it nearly impossible for her to look at even a picture of a snake.

The Effects of Emotions

Our emotions are vitally important to listen to and learn from. Each day you should strive to feel better than you felt at the beginning of the day. Even when you feel good, you should strive to feel really good.

Positive emotions such as joy indicate that you are on target with whatever you are thinking or focusing on. The thoughts you are creating, ideas you are pondering, and activities you are undertaking are actively moving you into the direction of your purpose, dreams, and desires.

In contrast, negative emotions such as anger, depression, or fear indicate that you are giving attention to those things that take you away from your dreams, hopes, or purpose. Incidentally, negative emotions may result in poor physical health. Scientific research shows that people who maintain a positive outlook during illness tend to show improvement or a delay in symptoms. Being conscious of why you feel what you feel is the key to dissolve build ups of negative energy.

The super conscious reveals to us not only what we should be excited about but it reveals the joy stealers that are present in our lives. The Bible declares in Isaiah 59:19 that when our enemies bombard our lives like floods that the Spirit of God raises a standard against them.

God is concerned about you feel. After all, it was He that created us to be emotional beings. Romans 14:17-18 states, "For the kingdom of God is not a matter of eating and drinking, but of righteousness, peace and joy in the Holy Spirit, because anyone who serves Christ in this way is pleasing to God and receives human approval." God's kingdom which is located within you is partly comprised of peace and joy which are two emotions. Maintaining an outlook of joy and peace not only is pleasurable to God but it causes people to admire you. People enjoy being in the company of positive people. Negative people are like vampires that drain you of your energy.

Spirit Led Emotions

The Holy Spirit empowers us to maintain a positive emotional state. Galatians 5:22-23 details what we call the fruit of the Spirit: love, joy, peace, forbearance, kindness, goodness, faithfulness, gentleness and self-control. These emotions are products of living life in higher Kingdom consciousness or living in the Spirit.

It is critical that we do not confuse our human emotions with the Holy Spirit. It is through faith that we access the powerful positive emotions of God when we are faced with life challenges. The Apostle Paul gives a great example of this in Philippians 4:11-13, "I am not saying this because I am in need, for I have learned to be content whatever the circumstances. I know what it is to be in need, and I know what it is to have plenty. I have learned the secret of being content in any and every situation, whether well fed or hungry, whether living in plenty or in want. I can do all this through him who gives me strength." Paul addresses the fact that he has faced many challenges during his ministry but he found the secret to contentment was controlling his emotional state.

Paul emphatically declares that he accomplishes this task through Christ, his strength. When we read of Christ, we discover that more than just the idea of Savior, He is the embodiment of perfect mind. Christ symbolizes the mind that is perfectly aligned with God having not embraced error but only spiritual truth. In your quest for wealth, health, peace and love, you must be conscious of your emotional state and the root cause of that state. Whatever is making you experience negative feelings must be appropriately dealt with such as anger, unforgiveness, rage, depression, hurt and so forth.

Unforgiveness Is Poison to Your Faith

Since I mentioned unforgiveness, you must know that it is poison to your faith. Unforgiveness is the greatest enemy of faith according to Mark 11:24-26 which states, "Therefore I tell you, whatever you ask for in prayer, believe that you have received it, and it will be yours. And when you stand praying, if you hold anything against anyone, forgive them, so that your Father in heaven may forgive you your sins." Unforgiveness is a prison that holds you limited and captive by the memory of someone that offended you. It only leads you to a life of bitterness and unsuccessful relationships when you are trapped by it. If your past is on your mind it is also in your future. More than likely, the person that offended you has moved on with their life and is giving no thought to what they did to you. Jesus Christ teaches us to forgive those who hurt us. Even Christ while dying on the cross prayed for the forgiveness of His executioners.

If you are struggling with unforgiveness, I suggest you take a piece of paper and write the name(s) of those people who offended you and their offenses. Then begin to pray and ask Jesus Christ to strengthen you to forgive those persons. Call each person's name and declare this prayer:

In the name of Jesus Christ I forgive (NAME) and release them from (CALL OUT THE OFFENSE). I declare that I am no longer bound by what they did against me. Jesus Christ I ask you to take their offense and nail them to the cross and do not hold it against them in the Day of Judgment. I declare I AM FREE, FREE, FREE, In Jesus Christ's name. Now take the paper and write on it I AM FREE seven times and throw it away. You may have to do this exercise more than once before it becomes your reality. Also, I encourage you to pray this prayer in the manner that is most comfortable to you.

CHAPTER FIVE

This book of the law shall not depart out of thy mouth; but thou shalt meditate therein day and night, that thou mayest observe to do according to all that is written therein: for then thou shalt make thy way prosperous, and then thou shalt have good success.
Joshua 1:8

LOVE: THE ELEVATOR OF HIGHER CONSCIOUSNESS

Love is the elevator to living on a higher level of consciousness. In fact, love is more than an emotion or attribute of God, it is His very nature. Scripture teaches us that God is love. In my opinion, love is entirely too precious to be given away, but love must be expressed. Love is the most powerful driving force in the kingdom of God. Love alone has the power to inspire, restore, heal, produce, create, nurture, and purge man.

The Law of Love is one of the greatest mysteries in the kingdom of God. Jesus Christ instituted the Law of Love as His final commandment to His disciples in John 14:34. The

Law of Love is that we unconditionally love others above ourselves having concern for their welfare and feelings. Walking in love releases you into the realm of absolute freedom because you are driven by desire to serve others. It is a miserable man who lives his entire life only to please himself without having compassion for other people. Whatever you produce in life will have an effect on future generations. Forward thinking people are driven by the power of love to create things that will better serve the world.

Human Love VS God's Love

Human love is conditional, while God's love is unconditional. People that operate on lower levels of consciousness usually express love to those that fulfill their personal desires. Selfish people think a lower level of consciousness being only aware of their personal wants and needs. Their aim is only to please them. As soon as they are not being pleased by others they have no further need for them. This type of selfish human love has left people abused, broken, and confused. Selfish people think on the levels of lower consciousness very similar animals being self gratifying also.

God's love is perfect in its essence. The Bible clearly describes for us how agape or unconditional love is expressed. In 1 Corinthians 13:4-8, it says, "Love is patient, love is kind. It does not envy, it does not boast, it is not proud. It does not dishonor others, it is not self-seeking, it is not easily angered, it keeps no record of wrongs. Love does not delight in evil but rejoices with the truth. It always protects, always trusts, always hopes, always perseveres. Love never fails." From this scripture, we learn that true unconditional love is an action.

> Love is the one system that will never fail.

Furthermore, love is constant and unchanging. The Scripture uses the word ALWAYS four times. God's love is not based upon what we do for Him. There is nothing anyone can do to earn God's love because His love is unfailing. When we are not loving to God, He still loves us, according to Romans 5:8 which tells us, "But God demonstrates his own love for us in this: While we were still sinners, Christ died for us." Even in a sinful state or condition, God's love for us is constant. An old cliché says, "God loves the sinner but he hates the sin."

Without God's love, there would be no salvation, healing, death and resurrection of Christ, reconciliation of man to God, or an afterlife. Each of those acts of God were orchestrated by His selfless love for man. John 3:16, states, "For God so loved the world that he gave his one and only Son, that whoever believes in him shall not perish but have eternal life." Love is so powerful that even the law of God and the Prophets are established upon it.

You Are the Expression of Divine Love

God expresses His love through us towards others. You and I are the conduits of God's perfect love on Earth. We are the hands of God to bring transformation to the lives that we are so blessed to touch. The true test for every disciple of Christ is that he or she is filled with love. Jesus said, in John 13:35, "that all mankind would know His disciples by the love they show to one another." When all of the spiritual gifts have ceased, only love will remain. Therefore, whatever you create must be fashioned in love. Your career, business, ministry, hopes and aspirations must be pursued in love.

Whatever your endeavor in life, you must love it and the people you will potentially serve. We have created a cosmic pollution of hate that affects the entire world through the matrix of collective consciousness. When we are properly aligned with the mind of God, our subconscious becomes a storehouse of loving thoughts.

A Life Pattern of Love

Our life patterns open doors for either negative or positive influences in our life. Many people talk about the love of God, but they do not know how to live it. You live love by releasing selfish desires and focusing on creating good that will benefit others. When you walk in love, you will maintain an attitude of abundance. Your mindset will be that there is enough room at the top for everyone and that you don't have to prove who you are. People that live in a higher level of consciousness don't feel they have a point to prove, but rather they simply express themselves. Your wealth, health, peace, and prosperity are expressions of your inner man. Remember, true success is first within, then without. There are many people who are outwardly successful but inward failures. You cannot think like God until you learn to love like God.

CHAPTER SIX

And set your minds and keep them set on what is above (the higher things), not on the things that are on the earth.
Colossians 3:2 AMP

THOUGHT--THE LANGUAGE OF CONSCIOUSNESS

Since all organic things have a level of consciousness, all things can communicate on the conscious on some level of thought. We must learn to speak the language of consciousness which is thought; to connect ourselves to understand all things, their needs and their relationship with humanity.

In order to understand how we speak on the conscious level, you must understand the law of thought. The law of thought is a universal principle that states that energy follows thought. Whatever you think about most is what will be created in your life.

A thought is a thing and attracts like energy to itself. Thoughts are biochemical electrical impulses that are measurable units of energy. In addition, thought waves have the ability to permeate time and space. One of the most important facts about your thoughts is that they can create physiological changes within your body. Negative thoughts are poisonous; they affect your body in many ways such as perspiration, muscular tension, weakened immune systems, and acidic environments. Cancer cells thrive in acidic environments.

Negative thoughts send out negative vibrations that attracts negative experiences in your life. In contrast, positive thoughts make you feel relaxed, more centered, and alert. They also attract positive experiences into your life. Do you know how powerful your thoughts are? Right thinking or righteousness will create right results in your life.

The thoughts that you think about most communicate with the conscious living world around you. Your thoughts are communicating with God at this present moment, creating events and opportunities that match them. I will explain this further in the chapter. Remember all things communicate on a conscious level. Just as you are communicating with things on Earth, you are equally communicating with things in Heaven. Humans think in terms of pictures; making it easier for people to learn visually.

All organic things communicate on some level of thought.

All of your thoughts form mental images in your conscious mind. When you choose to accept the image, it is then stored in your subconscious mind. The thoughts that you attach intense emotion to are the thoughts that pass through to subconscious storage. So the key to thoughts are not simply thinking about them but feeling strong about them. Your subconscious immediately goes to work to bring those images whether positive or negative that you feel strongest about into a reality.

Your subconscious projects these thoughts which are vibrational frequencies or resonance to the super conscious where all infinite possibilities are created. The resonance you project into the super conscious (mind of God) is indeed asking God to create what you are projecting. This happens because the frequencies you transmit only pair with like frequencies. The story I shared with you earlier about Job attracting into his life what he feared the most is a prime example.

Let me give you another example. Let's say you are overweight, and you desire to be thinner. Although, you may consciously prefer to be thin, subconsciously you hold an image of your being forever overweight; therefore, your subconscious mind will go to work to bring on more weight. Although, 1 John 3:2 says, "Beloved, I wish above all things that thou mayest prosper and be in health, even as thy soul prospereth," you will not experience it because subconsciously you do not believe you will have good health. The language of consciousness is thought and thought create your belief which influences your speech. Most of us have had embarrassing moments saying what we were thinking instead of what was prudent. In my example, I used weight but it correlates with money, relationships, or career and the list goes on and on. You create in your life according to the belief that you have internalized.

> Your subconscious belief system determines level of success you will achieve in life.

James 1:5-8 says, "But if any of you lacks wisdom, let him ask of God, who gives to all generously and without reproach, and it will be given to him. But he must ask in faith without any doubting, for the one who doubts is like the surf of the sea, driven and tossed by the wind. For that man ought not to expect that he will receive anything from the Lord, being a double-minded man, unstable in all his ways." This passage of Scripture tells us that we can ask for whatever we lack and God will give it to us generously. Now I want you to make it personal and instead of wisdom put what you lack in its place. This can be money, healthy lifestyle, customers, career growth the choice is yours.

The Scriptures instructs that you ask in faith without doubting in order to receive your request. This formula sounds simple and easy to follow doesn't it? So why haven't you manifested the thing that you asked for? Although you asked in faith consciously, however, subconsciously, you hold doubt that you will ever receive what you just asked for. Asking in faith is a conscious process; you reasoned and chose what you wanted. The only condition is that you can't doubt when you ask. If a doubt is stored in your subconscious, this causes a misalignment between your conscious and subconscious. As a result, a conflict has been created that has stopped you from manifesting the good that is held in the mind of God. It is your subconscious mind that communicates with your super conscious. The super conscious is unable to comprehend your desires that you are subconsciously doubtful of. The law of sowing and reaping begins to work and executes the demand that you receive what you've sown. Since doubt was sown more events will occur your life that validate the doubt. Think about it. You may doubt the abundant plan of God for your life because every event in your life up until now has given you reason to be uncertain. Here's the million dollar question, who projected the doubt that caused more reason to doubt, you or God? When you properly align your thought process with the mind of God; heaven will open up in your life.

CHAPTER SEVEN

But I say unto you, That every idle word that men shall speak, they shall give account thereof in the day of judgment.
Matthew 12:36

COMMUNICATING CONSCIOUSLY

The thoughts you hold in your mind are what you will verbally communicate to the world. Now that you understand the creative power of your thoughts, you will now consciously communicate the desires of your heart through your words. Your words are the building materials that create your life. The power of words enables you to step out on nothing and land on something. What you land upon is determined by whatever you spoke into existence. The old saying, "Sticks and stones may break my bones, but words will never hurt me," is one of the biggest lies we were ever taught.

Words are spiritual and creative; they are not simply sounds. Words impact our lives in so many different ways they can either encourage or discourage us. It's very obvious in the behavior of a child whose parents consistently affirm them with positive words. Usually those children are good students, are respectful, and confident in themselves. More than likely they will become successful because of the positive foundation laid in their life. Creation began with the word of God. Hebrews 11:3 NLV says, "By faith we understand that the entire universe was formed at God's command, that what we now see did not come from anything that can be seen." God created the entire universe through the speaking of his word.

Your Genesis Begins With Your Words

John 1:1-2,14A declares, "In the beginning was the Word, and the Word was with God, and the Word was God. He was with God in the beginning. The Word became flesh and made his dwelling among us..." The same goes for your personal genesis, meaning "a beginning," or "origin of anything." Your words initiate the beginning of the world you create for yourself. What you speak will manifest and dwell with you. Every human being possesses the same power of the spoken word. God is not separated from man. God dwells within man through spirit or consciousness. Therefore, the words we speak are empowered through the God nature within. The Bible teaches in John 6:63 that God's words are spirit and God's words are life. So, where does the power of life and death lie and who has the power? The answer is you have the power of life and death in your tongue. Proverbs 18:21 NLV states, "The tongue can bring death or life; those who love to talk will reap the consequences." According to the Scripture we can, and most often we do speak ourselves into negative situations. However, there is good news remember, God's words are spirit and are life.

> You have the power to name everything that is in your world

When Jesus taught His disciples about faith in Mark 11: 23,

He said, "Truly I tell you, if anyone says to this mountain, 'Go, throw yourself into the sea,' and does not doubt in their heart but believes that what they say will happen, it will be done for them." My argument isn't whether Jesus was referring to a literal or figurative mountain. However, I interpret this principle in this manner. According to Genesis, the earth was created by God's spoken words. So if words created mountains at the beginning of time then only words can remove the mountain. How many mountains have possibly been created in your life through negative talk? This means you must develop your faith vocabulary.

Develop Your Faith Vocabulary

Faith vocabulary means you must speak words that reinforce the good you want to experience in your life. The greatest dictionary and thesaurus for faith is the Bible, which is the written Word of God. Your faith vocabulary is developed by aligning your words with God's words. In other words, whatever is coming out of your mouth must be in agreement with the word of God.

Confessing God's word is necessary in order to receive the promises His word says. This is called the Law of Confession. Confession derives from the Greek word homologeo which is translated, to say the same thing as another.

Romans 9:9-10, says, "If you declare with your mouth, 'Jesus is Lord,' and believe in your heart that God raised him from the dead, you will be saved. For it is with your heart that you believe and are justified, and it is with your mouth that you profess your faith and are saved." Most often these Scriptures are used to lead a person into salvation. However, hidden within these Scriptures is the explanation of the power of confession.

The formula faith is the confession is made with your mouth and must be believed in your in your mind (heart). We believe in our minds (heart) and our faith is professed by our spoken words. For this reason, positive thinking alone doesn't fully manifest our desires into our lives.

Now, prophetic and emotional intelligence play a major part because we must know what to confess and how we feel about what we are confessing. As stated earlier, we receive intelligence from the super conscious, or the mind of God concerning our lives.

Your Test Is To Name Your World

During the genesis of life, at the dawn of creation, God gave Adam the privilege and responsibility to name all the animals He (God) created. This is found in Genesis 2:19, "Now the Lord God had formed out of the ground all the wild animals and all the birds in the sky. He brought them to the man to see what he would name them; and whatever the man called each living creature, that was its name."

How awesome. God allowed Adam to name all of the newly created animals. After moving past this amazement, I wondered, how did Adam know what to name all of the animals? After all, Adam was only a few hours old and there were no universities or books to draw from. My conclusion is that Adam was perfectly aligned with the mind of God or super conscious. God is omniscient, meaning He is all-knowing. Adam drew from the source of God's prophetic intelligence to accurately name all the animals as God had already named them. Therefore, the naming of the animals was a test of Adams alignment with God.

> Whoso keepeth his mouth and his tongue keepeth his soul from troubles.
>
> - Proverbs 21:23

Likewise, accurately naming all the good God has created for your life is your test of alignment with Him. God has already created every possible blessing for your life. Whatever you choose to name the blessing is what it will manifest as. From earlier in the book you may recall God's universal laws do not distinguish between what is wanted and unwanted from us. It is entirely up to us to execute the laws appropriately in our lives. Allow this to marinate in your spirit for a minute. Is it possible that you have been naming things wrongly in your life?

In Acts the 10th chapter, Peter called some food, God presented before him, unclean. In response, God said to Peter, "Do not call unclean what God has made clean." Anytime you speak negatively concerning your life, you are misnaming the things God has ordained for you.

The question to ask is, "How, or when do you curse your abundance?" Perhaps you are saying things in your life are hopeless when events do not go the way you prefer. Sometimes we complain about our jobs, family, financial status, and material possessions when they don't add up to desire. I'm not telling you to be content, but I am trying to help you frame your life by speaking positive powerful words. As a consequence, you must realize that your complaints are manifesting instead of your blessings because that is where your focus, emotions, and words are projected.

Let me explore some more biblical examples of what I am conveying to you about naming or calling blessings in your life. In Genesis 22, Abraham was faced with the daunting task of offering his son Isaac as a sacrifice. Reluctant, but yet obedient, Abraham follows through with God's request, tying Isaac to the altar to be sacrificed. However, before he could strike the deadly blow to Isaac, an angel called to him to stop and look over to see a ram trapped in the thicket to be used a sacrifice instead. In thanksgiving to God, Abraham named that place, "Jehovah Jireh," meaning, "the Lord will provide." Instead of complaining

> It's up to you to name the blessings in your life.

about going through the shock and mental anguish over almost losing his son, Abraham blessed the place by naming it Jehovah Jireh.

According to Genesis 29, we learn that Leah was one of Jacobs's two wives. Incidentally, his other wife was her sister Rachel. Leah had somewhat of a hard life. Apparently, she wasn't as attractive as her sister and didn't have many suitors for her hand in marriage. Jacob initially approached her father, Laban, to marry her younger sister Rachel, whom he loved. Laban agreed to the wedding but he tricked Jacob into marrying Leah, first. Jacob eventually married Rachel, but Leah suffered emotional abuse from this marriage. God lovingly blessed, Leah to become the mother of Jacob's first four sons. The Bible says God opened her womb because she was hated. Attempting to win her husband's affection she named the first three sons in correlation with how she expected Jacob's attitude to be changed towards her. She named her first son, Reuben, meaning the Lord has seen my affliction, now my husband will love me. Leah named her second son, Simeon, suggesting that the Lord heard she was unloved. Conceiving a third time, she named this son, Levi, declaring that now my husband will be attached to me. After three failed attempts at winning her husband's affections and adoration, she names her fourth son Judah, meaning, "Now, I will praise God." Leah is a prime example of a person who misnamed her blessings. She named all of her sons according to what she wanted from her husband. Finally, she let go of trying to please her husband and she shifted to pleasing God.

Although, it was quite unfortunate that she didn't fully receive her husband's attention, she was blessed to birth the first four sons of the twelve tribes of Israel. Likewise, you may be trying to manifest things in your life to please others or gain popularity. If so, you should know, God has blessed you with better for a greater purpose, but you are misnaming your blessings to serve the wrong purpose.

Your Mouth Is the Door of Success

The Bible tells us in Romans 4:17 that God called those things which are not as though they were. We, too, have this inherent power to manifest the spoken word. God calls things into existence with the frame of mind that they already exist.

The power of life and death are in your tongue and you will eat the fruit or the manifestation of what you speak. According to Proverbs 15:4, a wholesome tongue is a tree of life, meaning positive words give life to our lives. In Psalm 141:3 David prays, "Set a guard over my mouth, Lord; keep watch over the door of my lips." This means you have the responsibility to guard our own words. It is not God's responsibility to supervise what comes out of your mouth. On the contrary, it is your responsibility to take guard of your mouth and to be conscious of what you speak.

Jesus taught against unconsciously speaking. In Matthew 12:36, he said, "But I tell you that everyone will have to give account on the Day of Judgment for every empty word they have spoken." Psalm 19:14 records, "Let the words of my mouth, and the meditation of my heart, be acceptable in thy sight, O Lord, my strength, and my redeemer." You must consciously communicate in order to call forth the blessings in your life.

When you have experienced a shift into higher consciousness, it is imperative that you resist the urges to communicate on the levels of lower consciousness. The reason you must guard your words is found in Psalm 39:1. "I said, I will take heed to my ways, that I sin not with my tongue: I will keep my mouth with a bridle, while the wicked is before me." Satan and his demons are waiting to hear you speak the wrong things so they can bring them your life. The psalmist says

> Your mouth is the door way for your success.

he would put a bridle in his mouth to master his words. Paul teaches in Ephesians 4:29 "Let no corrupt communication proceed out of your mouth, but that which is good to the use of edifying, that it may minister grace unto the hearers." Be careful that you do not communicate negativity into your life.

Actually, you must learn how to keep your mouth closed and master the art of silence. Let's give notice to Proverbs 17:28, "Even a fool who keeps silent is considered wise; when he closes his lips, he is deemed intelligent." It is human nature to want to let off steam, but allow me to suggest to you instead of venting about your troubles, declare your faith in God's Word. Even Job confessed to God that he had spoken too much foolishly, as it is recorded in Job 40:1-4 (NLT), "Then the Lord said to Job, 'Do you still want to argue with the Almighty? You are God's critic, but do you have the answers?'"

Then Job replied to the Lord, "I am nothing—how could I ever find the answers? I will cover my mouth with my hand. I have said too much already. I have nothing more to say." The Scripture says those things we speak should minister grace or goodness to the hearer. Do you not realize that you actually listen to yourself speak? This is why confession of the Word of God is vital to living the abundant life. Faith comes by hearing and hearing by the Word of God. You will not have faith in what you have not heard. Let God be true, but every man a liar declares Romans 3:4. Allow the voice of God in you to be true and know that the flesh is a liar. Flesh is any nature that disagrees with the nature of God. Declare truth in your life and not lies. Anything that is opposite to what God has spoken concerning your life is a lie.

> God is speaking to you through thoughts, visions, or dreams.

Managing your words will help you avoid trouble according to Proverbs 21:23. Satan is so subtle, he uses the smallest moments to deceive us with our words. We often use sayings such as, "You scared me to death" or "This job is killing me." Even jokingly we speak negatively about other people and create negative events in their life. For instance, someone may be speeding and you might say, "That guy is going to kill himself." A few miles down the road the driver of the speeding vehicle has a terrible accident. That example is an exaggeration but it can happen.

The Word of God says in Ephesians 5:4, "Nor there be obscenity, foolish talk or coarse joking, which are out of place, but rather thanksgiving." Instead of making unwise unconscious statements about ourselves and others, let's consciously declare God's truth. There are times when the enemy will use negative circumstance and people to influence you to change your confession. Perhaps, you are calling things into your life that have not yet manifested. Beware of people who will challenge your faith and cause you to back up on your beliefs. Let me encourage you with this--the foolish man will never understand spiritual things. Declare that you are blessed and not cursed in the face of adversity.

Confess Deuteronomy 28:2-13

2 All these blessings will come on you and accompany
you if you obey the Lord your God:

3 You will be blessed in the city and blessed in the country.

4 The fruit of your womb will be blessed, and the crops of your land and the young of your livestock—the calves of your herds and the lambs of your flocks.
5 Your basket and your kneading trough will be blessed.

6 You will be blessed when you come in and blessed when you go out.

7 The Lord will grant that the enemies who rise up against you will be defeated before you. They will come at you from one direction but flee from you in seven.

8 The Lord will send a blessing on your barns and on everything you put your hand to. The Lord your God will bless you in the land he is giving you.

9 The Lord will establish you as his holy people, as he promised you on oath, if you keep the commands of the Lord your God and walk in obedience to him. 10 Then all the peoples on earth will see that you are called by the name of the Lord, and they will fear you. 11 The Lord will grant you abundant prosperity—in the fruit of your womb, the young of your livestock and the crops of your ground—in the land he swore to your ancestors to give you.

12 The Lord will open the heavens, the storehouse of his bounty, to send rain on your land in season and to bless all the work of your hands. You will lend to many nations but will borrow from none.

13 The Lord will make you the head, not the tail. If you pay attention to the commands of the Lord your God that I give you this day and carefully follow them, you will always be at the top, never at the bottom.

CHAPTER EIGHT

Let no corrupt communication proceed out of your mouth, but that which is good to the use of edifying, that it may minister grace unto the hearers.

Job 38:33

THE POWER OF FOCUS

Now you should have a greater awareness of how your mind and thoughts are creating your world at this very moment. In this chapter, I want to help you focus within so that you can receive the prophetic and emotional intelligence God is transmitting to you. You are now more aware of the kingdom of God and the vast resources that it has available for you. Actually, you are becoming a kingdom conscious person. It is vitally important that you consciously align yourself with the super conscious at the subconscious level. Remember, I used the words "mind of God" and "super conscious" interchangeably in this book.

Recall your attention to what God said concerning you in Jeremiah 29:11, "' For I know the plans I have for you,' declares the Lord, 'plans to prosper you and not to harm you, plans to give you hope and a future.'" God has good thoughts and plans for you. God wants you to know what those thoughts and plans are. You will never discover the divine plans of God for you if you do not quiet your mind to hear what the Spirit is speaking to you. We have all experienced moments of "knowing." These are those times when something told you, or perhaps you felt something would happen before it actually occurred. As earlier stated, we give these moments of knowing many labels such as intuition, prophetic, psychic, ESP, perception and so forth. These moments of knowing occur when you have settled down long enough to hear from the super conscious within.

Sadly, most people only pay attention to this voice of Spirit when it is speaking of danger. So how does this God speak? He is attempting to communicate to you, abundance, peace, and security for your life so that you will agree with them to manifest in your life. What does His voice sound like? This may shock you, but God's voice sounds absolutely nothing like it does in the movies. In 1 Kings 19:11-13 we learn what God's voice sounds like, "The Lord said, 'Go out and stand on the mountain in the presence of the Lord, for the Lord is about to pass by.' Then a great and powerful wind tore the mountains apart and shattered the rocks before the Lord, but the Lord was not in the wind. After the wind there was an earthquake, but the Lord was not in the earthquake. After the earthquake came a fire, but the Lord was not in the fire. And after the fire came a gentle whisper. When Elijah heard it, he pulled his cloak over his face and went out and stood at the mouth of the cave. Then a voice said to him, 'What are you doing here, Elijah?'

God didn't speak through the powerful wind, or the boisterous earthquake, neither in the luminous fire, He spoke in a quiet whisper. Stop waiting for huge dramatic moments for God to speak to you and turn within. God's presence is within you according to 1 Corinthians 3:16, 17, which states, "Don't you know that you yourselves are God's temple and that God's Spirit lives in you? If anyone destroys God's temple, God will destroy him; for God's temple is sacred, and you are that temple." You personally are the temple of God and He dwells in you. So if God dwells in us then why are we looking from without to hear what He is saying? Of course, God does speak to us through other people and occurrences. That is not my point; my point is to help you focus within to hear what God is speaking concerning you. I am recognized for my gift to share prophetic insight with others about their life. God speaks to me through thoughts and images about myself and other people. This is an ability that we all possess in one particular measure. In 1 Corinthians 14:5, the Apostle Paul admonishes us to desire the ability to prophecy.

I do not believe it is the will of God for anyone to live without knowing what their life's purpose is. Success is found when you realize your purpose and you live each day fulfilling that purpose. We are extensions of the power of God in the universe. It is imperative that you make the decision today to consciously tap into the mind of God to not only know your purpose, but know how you will fulfill your purpose.

Step One - Watch Your Thoughts

You must become the watcher of your thoughts by becoming a master of focus. Focus is your tool to attract into your life the good things that are awaiting you in the mind of God. The law of thought states that what you focus on the most is what will manifest in your life. Thoughts are electrical impulses that are charged with either positive or negative emotions. My intention is not to be redundant, but I want to make certain that you remember these universal laws and principles. Jesus said in John 14:6, "I am the way and the truth and the life. No one comes to the Father except through me." This means that Jesus is firstly the path to travel as well as the ultimate example of how you should conduct yourself on the journey. Secondly, when He says the truth, He has provided for us to have purity of mind. Lastly, Jesus fulfilled the purpose that we may have life and live it more abundantly. Nothing outside of Jesus' example of being the way, truth, and life can access the mind of God. I am now going to lay out a process that you can implement to become a focus master.

One of my favorite Scriptures about thought is Philippians 4:8-9, "Finally, brothers, whatever is true, whatever is noble, whatever is right, whatever is pure, whatever is lovely, whatever is admirable—if anything is excellent or praiseworthy—think about such things. Whatever you have learned or received or heard from me, or seen in me—put it into practice. And the God of peace will be with you." You must pay attention to what you are thinking about. If what you are thinking about most of the time does not fit in any one of the categories, it then must be dissolve. That negative thought is creating a reality for you that you actually do not want. Your mind is like a movie theater. Therefore, you must step out of the film that is playing and take a seat in the audience to observe what is playing. I do this anytime my day is going sour, or I am really annoyed for no apparent reason. I become the observer of my thoughts and when I realize the thought that is creating the negativity in my "Now," I stop it by replacing it with the positive God has spoken.

Step Two - Apprehend Negative Thoughts

This leads me to the next step in the process which is apprehend the negative thought. We don't want to waste time judging ourselves for the negative thought or even scrutinizing it. We must simply move it or delete it, from the film of our life. 2 Corinthians 10:4-5 (AMP), states, "For the weapons of our warfare are not physical [weapons of flesh and blood], but they are mighty before God for the overthrow and destruction of strongholds, [Inasmuch as we] refute arguments and theories and reasonings and every proud and lofty thing that sets itself up against the [true] knowledge of God; and we lead every thought and purpose away captive into the obedience of Christ (the Messiah, the Anointed One)." Demonic strongholds are demonically-induced patterns of thought. Your mind is the household of thought. Any thought that you have that goes against the thoughts of God concerning you are demonic in nature. The devil is the attacker of your mind. When you emotionally embrace a negative thought as truth for your life, it creates a stronghold or dwelling place for Satan in your mind. So today you will evict him by taking his negative thought captive and commanding it to become obedient to the presence of Christ in your life. Jesus Christ is the Messiah, the Anointed One that has broken every chain and shackle that attempts to keep you bound. When negative thoughts are brought into the presence of Christ, it has to conform to what God has already spoken.

Step Three - Consciously Meditate

Conscious meditation is the next step in your process of being a focus master. Psychology has proven that our brains are only able to think one thought at a time. Since your brain has the capacity to focus only on one particular thought at a time, you much choose what you will think about. The power of focus is conscious meditation. Conscious meditation is you choosing to focus your mind on one thought, idea, or mantra about what God has said concerning you. Spending time focusing on the word of God will result in the renewal of your mind. Go beyond renewing your conscious mind by beginning renewal at the subconscious mind level. Your subconscious mind is the spirit of your mind having the innate ability to commune with the super conscious.

Ephesians 4:23 says, "be renewed in the spirit of your mind." Remove yourself from the mediocre existence that average people settle for. Again mind renewal is an essential process to do this according to Romans 12:2 "Do not conform any longer to the pattern of this world, but be transformed by the renewing of your mind. Then you will be able to test and approve what God's will is--his good, pleasing and perfect will."

Meditation is not a time for talking, but a time for listening from within. You are quieting your mind, releasing the cares, fears, or anxieties that are discomforting you, to turn within to hear what God's Spirit is speaking. Jesus said in the book of Revelations, he that has an ear let him hear what the Spirit is saying. The time you spend in meditation will develop your ear to hear what the Spirit is expressing.

Take time to meditate for a few minutes on the word of God manifesting itself concerning your life. Conscious meditation will take you into the "secret place of the most high" (Psalm 91). God's word is communicated in two forms which are Logos and Rhema. The Logos word is the written expressions of God that we find in the Bible. These written words are the authority on God's plan for your life. The Rhema word is the divinely revealed word of God that comes in the forms of prophetic thoughts and expressions. Joshua 1:8 says, "This book of the law shall not depart out of thy mouth; but thou shalt meditate therein day and night, that thou mayest observe to do according to all that is written therein: for then thou shalt make thy way prosperous, and then thou shalt have good success." Good success will come into your life through conscious meditation.

> Your true enemy is never a person but rather any thought that attacks your mind.

Take 10 to 15 minutes, sitting in a comfortable place where you will not be disturbed. Allow yourself to focus on each breath that you take until your body is completely relaxed. Focus your thoughts only on a Scripture, Psalm, or an affirmation while you are meditating. You will notice that your mind will tend to wander, and that is to be expected. Simply bring your mind back into focus on the word. Your meditation time should never become strenuous work for you; this is a time where you posture yourself to become one with Spirit.

Meditation is also a practice that you can use to solve problems. If you are facing a problem do not focus on the problem but rather focus on this affirmation: "God has provided a solution for the problem. I am one with the mind of God and receive revelation about this problem now. Thank you God in me for the solution." You may use whatever affirmation or mantra that you are comfortable with.

Step Five - Strategic Prayer

Strategic Prayer is the next step in becoming a focus master. Prayer is the currency of the kingdom of God. When you engage in prayer, you are in communion with the Father. Prayer is the birthing room for the plan of God for your life. I do not have time to tell you in this book how many things have worked favorably in my life because I executed the power of prayer. In her book, The Power of Prospering Prayer, Catherine Ponder wrote, "The person who truly prays is bound to succeed because he attunes himself to the richest, most powerful, most successful force in the universe." (Ponder, 1983)

You must discipline yourself to become a person of prayer. Praying people always prosper. When Jesus was praying in the Garden of Gethsemane, He was disappointed in His disciples because they could not stay awake to pray for one hour. Are you like those disciples that you cannot stay focused long enough to pray about your life? Jesus instructed

His disciples to pray so that they would not fall into temptation. These instructions remain true for us today.

I often pondered why Jesus picked the Garden of Gethsemane to pray. There were so many other significant places in Jerusalem that Jesus could have prayed. Jesus prays in the Garden of Gethsemane because it was in the Garden of Eden where Satan tempted Adam and Eve, consequently, stealing dominion from them.

The garden is a very significant place spiritually in the Bible. The garden represents the spiritual body in which man dwells when he brings forth thoughts after the pattern of original divine ideas. Spiritually, your mind and spirits are types of gardens where seeds of thoughts create patterns in your life. Equally, as God sows seeds within you, Satan also can sow seeds within your mind and spirit, as well. Satan's seeds become strongholds within the mind of an individual. Remember, a stronghold may be defined as a demonically-influenced pattern of thought.

Patterns of thought influence our daily actions that develop into life habits. Moreover, whoever is in control of the garden has the control of the harvest that it produces. Satan tempted Adam and Eve to reject the original plan of God in an attempt to gain control of what was produced from the garden. Adam and Eve were evicted from Eden as the result of their falling into temptation.

Eden means pleasure or delightful paradise. Whenever, you allow negative thoughts to contradict the abundant thoughts of God, you will be evicted from your personal paradise. Therefore, Jesus instructs the disciples to pray so that they would not enter into temptation. You must not yield

Successful people throughout the ages have developed their intuitive muscles.

to the temptation of doubt, fear, or unbelief they will cause disruption in your personal Eden.

Nothing will take place in your life until you pray it through first. It is vital that you pray over the things God has promised to bless you with until you see them come to manifestation. This type of prayer is called prophetic intercession.

In prophetic intercession, you do not pray according to what you want or think about something but rather your prayer is empowered by a vision, word, or inspiration that God has spoken to you. Prophetic intercession is a spiritual warfare method used to guard your promises until they arrive at your front door. When you pray, you must believe you have received what you asked for without any doubt.

Philippians 4:6 tells us, "Do not be anxious about anything, but in everything, by prayer and petition, with thanksgiving, present your requests to God. Whatever you are expecting to receive from the God you must first present it in prayer. When I teach students about prayer I always tell them to stop praying all over heaven. This means having unfocused prayers and calling things out at random. On the contrary, your prayer must be strategic and specific about your life, business, ministry, marriage, etc. Allow me to suggest that you write out the things you desire to take place in your life and pray concerning each one of them. Do not do all of the talking when you pray, but also allow God to speak concerning what you are asking for. The fact is what you are asking for may actually be out of sync with what God has planned for you. You may be thinking, but Richard you said I could have whatever I desire. This is partially true, however, if what you desire violates the laws or principles of God, then your request will be denied. For instance, if you want to marry your neighbor's spouse you cannot pray to God to bless you to marry that person. That would absolutely violate God's principles concerning marriage. James 4:3, "When you ask, you do not receive, because you ask with wrong motives, that you may spend what you get on your pleasures." If your motives are wrong you will never receive them from God. Anyway, God has far greater for us that we could ever think, ask, or imagine (Ephesians 3:20).

Step Six – Live Like You Got It

Finally, you must act as if you already have what you are focused on. You assume the consciousness of what you desire when you live as if you already own what you desire. Do not wait until you become a CEO; or in a loving relationship; or have lots of money, or healed from a disease. Act as if you have it before you get it. Sometimes you have to fake it until you make it. It is an act of faith for you to behave as if your prayer has been physically answered. Your conversation, mannerisms, and attitude should all exemplify the level of higher consciousness you have risen to. You will cause your subconscious mind to believe you already have what you are waiting on. In return, your subconscious mind will project the image you are presenting that will result in its manifestation. When the Israelites were convinced they couldn't possess the Promised Land because it was inhabited by giants, Caleb spoke up and said, "Let us go up at once, and possess it; for we are well able to overcome it." Caleb acted as if he had the victory before he even possessed the land. It didn't matter to Caleb whether the people were right or wrong about not being able to conquer the land because he had already conquered it in his mind. A vision will sustain you in your difficult times. When you change the way you think then you will change what you say.

All creation begins with a thought. This is God's original process for creation. When God created the heavens and the earth he first conceived it as a thought; then He believed it. God spoke it, and it manifested into a creation. This process works for you, as well. You must first conceive an idea (have hope), then believe it (provide faith for it), speak it (call it into existence) and it will manifest. Where did the thought come from? It came from a spiritual source which is the mind of God or the influence of Satan. God created the heavens and the earth, and then he gave us the ability to continue the creation process. All inventions, ministries, buildings, science, art, schools, companies, relationships, etc., first began as a thought. Their creator had to experience an epiphany or inspiration that led to their creation. All creations that promote good are divinely inspired from the mind of God.

Therefore, you must be aligned with God's mind in order to know the strategy to create what He has for you. Your alignment is your agreement with God's plans for your life. The agreement will cause heaven to open over your life. In my personal life, I have used this process to manifest cars, fur coats, money, jobs, key friendships, scholarships, ministry opportunities, clients, relocation and my beautiful wife. Believe it or not this exact process manifested this book into existence. I have been prophesied to for years by many people that I would write a book. This year I declared that I would release my first book by a certain date. I was developing a training manual for a Christian Marketplace Conference and within less than a week I had written five chapters of this book.

Hear me clearly; I was not born with a silver spoon in my mouth although I come from a wonderful family. I wasn't the guy that all the cheerleaders wanted to date as far as I know. When I became dissatisfied with my world I restructured my belief system. I began to focus my mind on the infinite possibilities of abundance that God has for me. These principles have worked for me, and they will certainly work for you. The principles will work if you work them.

CHAPTER NINE

Let them shout for joy, and be glad, that favour my righteous cause: yea, let them say continually, Let the LORD be magnified, which hath pleasure in the prosperity of his servant.
Psalm35:27

PORTALS TO AN OPEN HEAVEN

Many people profess to hear from God. Some of these people have committed heinous acts because they were convinced God told them to do so. I've coached people who told me that God told them to do something and it turned out to be disastrous. God's blessing gives us increase and do not bring any sorrow into our lives. My all-time favorite is when someone says God told them to do one thing and then the story changes two days later. All of these individuals have been deceived by some other influence that has disguised itself as God. You cannot or will not hear the voice of God without the presence of God. Just think of it in natural terms. Can someone hold a conversation with you who isn't present with you, whether face to face, telephone, Skype, or by some other technology? This brings up the question, how can I have the presence of God to hear the voice of God?

The Spirit revealed to me a step-by-step process from the scriptures to open heaven in my life. What is an open Heaven? An open heaven is an uninterrupted manifestation of the presence of God in your life. The presence of heaven in your life will cause all natural laws to cease permanently or temporarily. Supernatural signs and wonders such as healings, miracles, accelerations, angelic visitations, and revelations will manifest in your life. When heaven is opened over your life, there will be an out pour of His power and blessings upon your life, family, ministry, business, etc. There is a wealth transfer that is taking place but it is only happening to those who remain under an open heaven. You must have heaven to open because this is where all of your spiritual blessings are located according to Ephesians 1:3 which states, "Blessed be the God and Father of our Lord Jesus Christ, who hath blessed us with all spiritual blessings in heavenly places in Christ:" This sounds so wonderful but most people will not do what is necessary to command heaven to open up for them. Isaiah 64:11 tells us, "Oh that thou wouldest rend the heavens, that thou wouldest come down, that the mountains might flow down at thy presence."

Heaven won't open up for you just because you have your name on the church membership list. Singing and shouting alone will not open heaven in your life. You may not realize that you are possibly living in an area where heaven is actually closed up. This is called living under a hard heaven. Consider Deuteronomy 28:23: "And thy heavens that is over thy head shall be brass, and the earth under thee shall be iron. The Lord shall make the rain of thy land powder and dust: from heaven shall it come down upon thee, until thou be destroyed." Believe it or not, your ministry, business, job, or home is more than likely in an area where heaven is closed and hard. It is very frustrated to be located in an area were heaven is closed up. Man's sin causes heaven to close up over them. Therefore, you must engage heaven to command it to open. This is the season that you must put some pressure on heaven to command it to open up for you. Although heaven may be closed in a region, your relationship with God can command it to open up for you. Let me give you an example of experiencing an open heaven when your area is under a hard heaven from Exodus 10:21-23: "And the Lord said unto Moses, Stretch out thine hand toward heaven, that there may be darkness over the land of Egypt, even darkness which may be felt. And Moses stretched forth his hand toward heaven; and there was a thick darkness in all the land of Egypt three days: They saw not one another, neither rose any from his place for three days: but all the children of Israel had light in their dwellings."

The children of Israel were enslaved in Egypt and God performed acts that would force the hand of Pharaoh to emancipate them. God released such a gross darkness on Egypt that it could be felt. While all of Egypt was covered in great darkness, the children of Israel had light where they lived in Goshen. So we see Heaven can open over you for a supernatural release of power while the rest of your area is under a brass heaven. Your open heaven experience can cause transformation in such major way in your area of influence. People will begin to ask how you are prospering while the rest of the city is in distress. This will be your moment to manifest as the glory of God to show forth his power.

Prepare your heart to experience an open heaven as I lay out this biblical step-by-step process for you. God begin to open my eyes to a greater revelation of a very familiar event in the Bible from 1 Kings 18, that is Elijah's confrontation with the Prophets of Baal on Mt. Carmel You can apply each one these principles in your life that will radically command heaven to open in your life.

Principle One: Make A Decision (1 Kings 18:21)

21And Elijah came unto all the people, and said, How long halt ye between two opinions? if the Lord be God, follow him: but if Baal, then follow him. And the people answered him not a word.

Indecisiveness is one of the greatest hindrances to your productivity. This entire process is a mental process that must take place in your mind first. In Matthew 4:17, Jesus began to preach repent for the kingdom of Heaven is at hand. Repent comes from the Greek word metanoeō which means change your mind. When Jesus preached repentance in this passage of Scripture, He was saying that we must first have a change of our mindset before we can experience the kingdom. Elijah uses the word opinion. Where are your opinions located? You opinions are located in your mind. Whatever you are stuck between is a stronghold that is in your mind first. A stronghold is a demonically-induced pattern of thought. Satan does not create strongholds in our minds; we do. Satan sits in the stronghold because we establish the stronghold with negative energy.

People have such a difficult time in making concrete decisions for their lives. Many have, according to the old phrase, "too many irons in the fire." The only way you will become successful is by making a decision about what you are truly passionate about. Making this type of decisions is very tough for multi-talented people. You want to be a singer, actor, business mogul, and minister all at the same time. Truthfully, you may be great in each one of these areas but you are only most passionate about one. Successful people only focus on one area at time. Decide on your passionate path and maximize your opportunities in that area. You will begin to notice how your other gifts and talents will compliment your passion. You may even realize that you have been focusing on an assignment that has expired in your life. Did I just say that? Yes, I did! There are times when our aspirations expire because of our procrastination in fulfilling them. Elijah question to the people is being asked of you right now. How long will you remain stagnate between two opinions? Perhaps you have been standing still in a safe place which is a state of being, but it is time for you to start becoming who you have been destined to become. The process of becoming never ends. We are always evolving from one dimension to the next. Make a decision concerning who you will become at this very moment.

After making the first decision in becoming, you must establish a strong belief system to support the process. This means that you must develop your faith in God or remain unstable in your faith. Your instability in faith is actually blocking the manifestation of God's power in your life. Right now, health, wealth, peace, and prosperity are running to you, but one thought of doubt causes them to retreat. James 1:6-8 explains to us that God will not honor faith that is wavering.

Have you met people who have been in every network marketing business under the sun? I've watch these people, and I have noticed that they are never successful in any of those businesses. I have seen ministers who changed their focus constantly. One day God has called them to pastor but after a few months of no growth they switch to evangelism. Sometimes, they even change the messages that they preach. First they preach the word of faith message, but when nothing happens for them, they begin to preach deliverance messages. When there still isn't any growth in the ministry, they switch from deliverance to kingdom messages.

Don't get me wrong, God will give us new revelations but you do not have to reinvent yourself because something isn't growing fast enough. Your constant switching from business to business, ministry to ministry, gimmick to gimmick is evidence of your lack of faith. You must continue in your passion with sure confidence that will increase your efforts. I could say so much more about this, but I will wait until my next book. Declare that this is your defining moment, and you are making a definite decision about the will of God for your life. James 1:6-8 But let him ask in faith, nothing wavering. For he that wavereth is like a wave of the sea driven with the wind and tossed. 7For let not that man think that he shall receive any thing of the Lord. 8A double minded man is unstable in all his ways.

Principle Two: Be A Specialist In Your Field

1 Kings 18:22-24Then said Elijah unto the people, I, even I only, remain a prophet of the Lord; but Baal's prophets are four hundred and fifty men. .Let them therefore give us two bullocks; and let them choose one bullock for themselves, and cut it in pieces, and lay it on wood, and put no fire under: and I will dress the other bullock, and lay it on wood, and put no fire under: And call ye on the name of your gods, and I will call on the name of the Lord: and the God that answereth by fire, let him be God. And all the people answered and said, It is well spoken.

Elijah boldly declares that he was the only prophet of the Lord that remained after Jezebel had massacred the other prophets. Now this statement was quite bold because Obadiah had hidden 150 prophets in a cave. Was Elijah lying to the prophets of Baal? On the contrary, I believe he was asserting that he was the only prophet equipped to confront the 450 prophets of Baal.

Elijah then proves himself as a prophetic specialist because he knew exactly what to do in this time of crisis. It is so embarrassing for someone to make bold claims that they are unable to validate. Of course, you are not the only person in your industry, but you must declare yourself the specialist or an expert in your field.

There is a spiritual law that you must learn that is call the Law of I AM. We are introduced to the Law of I Am in Exodus 3:13-14: 13And Moses said unto God, Behold, when I come unto the children of Israel, and shall say unto them, The God of your fathers hath sent me unto you; and they shall say to me, What is his name? What shall I say unto them? 14And God said unto Moses, I AM THAT I AM: and he said, Thus shalt thou say unto the children of Israel, I AM hath sent me unto you. I AM is God's definition of Himself declaring that He is whatever is required. I AM is God, and it is His name.

We have the nature of I AM within us. The I AM nature is our power to create and to become. Each time we say I am we are taking the name of the Lord. God commands us not to take the name of the Lord in vain. Every mind takes the name of the Lord whether conscious, unconscious, or subconscious. Each time you add a negative to I AM you take the name of the Lord in vain.

Jesus declared at least twenty seven I AM statements between the books of John and Revelation. Whatever is added to I AM is what He became in that instant-- I AM the bread of life, I AM the resurrection, or I AM the true vine. Joel 3:10 declares, "Beat your plowshares into swords, and your pruninghooks into spears: let the weak say, I am strong." Whatever you add to I AM you become because it is a spiritual law.

You cannot become what you have not yet seen. The process of becoming begins with a mental image first. Imagination is the digital camera of our mind because we think in terms of pictures. The subconscious mind does not discern between the real and fake images. Therefore, you are becoming whatever images you are projecting, and those images become your thoughts. Those thoughts then manifest themselves into things in your life.

Elijah stood out as an expert in the field of prophets when he said "I, even I only." At that moment, God equipped him with the prophetic strategy to confront Baal's prophets. There is no need for you to feel that you need to fit in with everyone else. You need to stand in a class all by yourself.

My wealth mentor would often say to me "playing small doesn't serve the world." Playing small isn't making you any money or getting you any closer to your God-ordained success. People only want to hear from an expert. Affirm the law of I AM in your life right now. Declare I AM MONEY! I AM HEALED! I AM PROSPEROUS! I AM LOVED!

Principle Three: Gather Your Crowd

1 Kings 18:30A And Elijah said unto all the people, Come near unto me. And all the people came near unto him.

Earlier, I shared with you how prophetic intelligence will make you influential. How could Elijah gather the audience to him if he didn't have any influence? Remember this group of people also worshipped Baal along with God, therefore, something about Elijah's presence attracted the people to him. Heaven will open up for you when you become influential in your field. After all, God is looking for opportunities to prove His presence and power in your life so others will be drawn to your witness. 2 Chronicles 16:9 declares, "For the eyes of the Lord run to and fro throughout the whole earth, to shew himself strong in the behalf of them whose heart is perfect toward him." Your success in life is a witness to those that do not know the power of God.

Elijah was a risk-taker. He made great claims of the power of God in front of his enemies. He taunted them by making fun of their god and his lack of response to them. Elijah was one man in the midst of 450 prophets of Baal, but he still remained steadfast in his faith. Like Elijah, you must stand for something--choose what side of the fence you are on. Influential people are known for what they stand for, and this is one of the reason people stand with them.

People will only follow leaders they can see, leaders who are present. You cannot influence people from behind; you must be in the forefront. You must be seen everywhere. How can you do this? I know you are asking this question. Use technology to your advantage by directing people to your work, business, or ministry through social media, blogs, etc. Network, network, and network! In our effort to be spiritual, many of us sit at home and say to ourselves God will make a way, or God will open doors. Stop using spiritual clichés as an excuse for your fear to get out there and speak for yourself. Develop a network of people you can partner with in efforts that mutually serve each other. Find people that do the opposite of what you do because you can learn something new to develop yourself. You will never become influential if you cannot connect with people.

Influential people take actions that will cause people to react. Elijah responds to the prophets of Baal in such a way that the people gathered had no choice but to react. You must not be afraid of the reaction that the public will give to you. Some people will agree and others will disagree. The intention is to gain the attention of your audience.

Principle Four: Repair Your Prayer Altar

1 Kings 18:30B And he repaired the altar of the Lord that was broken down.

Prayer is the currency of the kingdom of God. Nothing will happen in your life until you pray it out first. Everything that comes into the earth must be born into the earth. Even Jesus in His divinity didn't just show up in Bethlehem as a grown man saying, "Shalom, Ya'll." He was born into the earth. Prayer is the incubator to manifest your dreams and visions into your life. When Jesus taught on faith in Mark 11:24 24, He said, "I say unto you, "What things soever ye desire, when ye pray, believe that ye receive them, and ye shall have them." He correlates prayer with your faith. Your desires must first be presented to God in prayer. However, prayer alone will not get you an answer; you must believe that you have received the things you prayed about.

Prayer is one of the tools that will open up a hard heaven over your life. 2 Chronicles 7:13-15 says, "If I shut up heaven that there be no rain, or if I command the locusts to devour the land, or if I send pestilence among my people; If my people, which are called by my name, shall humble themselves, and pray, and seek my face, and turn from their wicked ways; then will I hear from heaven, and will forgive their sin, and will heal their land. Now mine eyes shall be open, and mine ears attentive unto the prayer that is made in this place." God's solution to open to hard heavens over the land is prayer. The lack of prayer is what is holding up heaven opening in your life. Maybe you have been praying. However, you may be missing some key ingredients to successful prayer. Your prayers must first be aligned with the will of God. You may argue that Mark 11:24 that says you can pray for the things you desire. That's a good point, but let's go deeper in the word of God about desires. James 4:3 says, "Ye ask, and receive not, because ye ask amiss, that ye may consume it upon your lusts." Your prayers must first in accordance with the will of God. You can pray for a spouse, but you can't pray that a married person will divorce their spouse to marry you. It is perfectly fine to pray that God will bless you with money, but God will not bless you with money to go after lustful pleasures. Your desires must be holy. Psalm 37:4 states, "Delight yourself in the Lord, and he will give you the desires of your heart." As you delight or find pleasure in the presence of God, your desires will transform into what God desires for you. Guess what friend? What God desires for you is far greater than what you could ever want for yourself.

This leads me to the importance of praying in the Spirit. Romans 8: 26-27 tells us, "Likewise the Spirit also helpeth our infirmities: for we know not what we should pray for as we ought: but the Spirit itself maketh intercession for us with groanings which cannot be uttered. And he that searcheth the hearts knoweth what is the mind of the Spirit, because he maketh intercession for the saints according to the will of God." This teaches us the secret to successful prayer. The secret to successful prayer really isn't a secret but most people do not do it. Successful prayer is Spirit-led prayer.

Our infirmity or weakness is that we do not know what to pray for ourselves. Therefore, the Holy Spirit makes intercession and prays through us according to the will of God for our lives. Praying in tongues is a biblical practice for praying in the Holy spirit. When we pray in our native language we are praying what we know but when you pray in tongues you are praying the perfect will of God. I encourage you to pray in your heavenly language (providing you have that spiritual gift) every day so that you will pray according to the will of God. I am in no way saying that your prayers are irrelevant if you do not pray in tongues. God understands our prayer in any language. However, I am sharing with you a more dynamic approach in your prayer life. Also, praying in the Spirit builds up your spirit man. Joel 2:20, states, "But ye, beloved, building up yourselves on your most holy faith, praying in the Holy Ghost." This further takes us into the reality that prayer without the Holy Spirit will always be unsuccessful. Romans 8:28, which is many people's favorite Scriptures assures us that all things will work out for our good only after spirit-led prayer.

Principle Five: Put Your Life in Order

1 Kings 18:30 And Elijah took twelve stones, according to the number of the tribes of the sons of Jacob, unto whom the word of the Lord came, saying, Israel shall be thy name:

Heaven will not open up for you until you put your life in order. You must prioritize your life based upon what is important. Elijah took 12 stones representing the tribes of Israel to build his alter. Twelve is the biblical number that symbolizes government foundation, divine authority, or completeness. There are 12 tribes of Israel; 12 people anointed in the Bible to serve in government, Jesus chose 12 disciples, and the church began with 12 Apostles. Government foundation is significant to structure and accountability. Structure and accountability are a must in your life for heaven to open up. Develop clear goals and plans for your life that you can refer to as a map for yourself. The US Government has a system of checks and balances in place. Create a system for checks and balances in your life by finding a coach, mentor, pastor or someone that will hold you accountable in accomplishing your goals. Successful people remain teachable and coachable so they can reach the next level in their lives.

Principle Six: Sow and Reap

1 Kings 18:33 And he put the wood in order, and cut the bullock in pieces, and laid him on the wood, and said, Fill four barrels with water, and pour it on the burnt sacrifice, and on the wood.

The greatest power that you have to open heaven is the power of the seed offering. Acts 10:31 says, "And said,

Cornelius, thy prayer is heard, and thine alms are had in remembrance in the sight of God." This Scripture is so important because it show us that our seed completes our faith. Cornelius was a generous Gentile who had been earnestly praying to God for something.

An angel visits him to let him know that not only his prayers, but his offerings were a memorial in the sight of God. Not only is there a record of your prayers in heaven but also a record of your giving in heaven. Genesis 26:12 says, "Then Isaac sowed in that land, and received in the same year an hundredfold: and the Lord blessed him." Isaac did not reap the harvest of the land that God had sent him into until he planted his seed. Perhaps you've been in that business or ministry that God showed you all of this time and have seen the blessings of your obedience. You might have given offerings and paid your tithes. The question is, however, did you give the seed that God told you to give? If you didn't give the seed that God told you to give, then you have given the wrong seed. Your harvest will never manifest until you sow the appropriate seed. God does not give us things but He gives us seed that will manifest into what we need.

In the beginning, God spoke everything into existence until He got the creation of the garden. Genesis 2:8 states, "And the Lord God planted a garden eastward in Eden; and there he put the man whom he had formed." God planted the garden with seed and then He gave seed to man to grow whatever he needed. Genesis 1: 29 tells us, "And God said, Behold, I have given you every herb bearing seed, which is upon the face of all the earth, and every tree, in the which is the fruit of a tree yielding seed; to you it shall be for meat."

Everything you will ever desire on earth is hidden in your seed. Heaven will never open over the lives of people who are not givers. Your financial offering is the only seed that has the ability to grow into another form. Apple seed only yields apples; orange seed only yields oranges, but your money seed can yield a house, car, new career, business, debt relief, you name it. 2 Corinthians 9:6-8 says, "But this I say, He which soweth sparingly shall reap also sparingly; and he which soweth bountifully shall reap also bountifully. Every man according as he purposeth in his heart, so let him give; not grudgingly, or of necessity: for God loveth a cheerful giver. And God is able to make all grace abound toward you; that ye, always having all sufficiency in all things, may abound to every good work." If you want to receive a bountiful harvest or in laymen's terms, "a whole bunch of stuff," you must give bountifully.

So where should you sow your seed? I am so glad you ask this question. First of all, you should sow your seed where you are being spiritually taught. Galatians 6:10 AMP tells us, "Let him who receives instruction in the Word [of God] share all good things with his teacher [contributing to his support]." Allow me to reemphasize you should financially support whomever is teaching you the spiritual principles. Secondly, God has promised to bless those who bless the poor in Psalm 41:1. It reads, "Blessed is he that considereth the poor: the Lord will deliver him in time of trouble." This is a spiritual principle that will work for you. If you find your business or ministry in trouble such as financial, give faithfully to the poor. Giving to the poor will cause angelic assistance to come to your immediate aide as we learned in Acts Chapter 10 from Cornelius.

Last, but not least, you must pay your tithe which is ten percent of your earnings. Tithing is holy, and it has nothing to do with the Law of Moses. God had established tithing before He gave Moses the law. Malachi 3:8-12 declares, "Will a man rob God? Yet ye have robbed me. But ye say, Wherein have we robbed thee? In tithes and offerings. Ye are cursed with a curse: for ye have robbed me, even this whole nation. Bring ye all the tithes into the storehouse, that there may be meat in mine house, and prove me now herewith, saith the Lord of hosts, if I will not open you the windows of heaven, and pour you out a blessing, that there shall not be room enough to receive it. And I will rebuke the devourer for your sakes, and he shall not destroy the fruits of your ground; neither shall your vine cast her fruit before the time in the field, saith the Lord of hosts. And all nations shall call you blessed: for ye shall be a delightsome land, saith the Lord of hosts." Your tithe will break the back of poverty to keep it away from your life.

Principle Seven: Timing Is Everything

1 Kings 18:36 And it came to pass at the time of the offering of the evening sacrifice, that Elijah the prophet came near, and said, Lord God of Abraham, Isaac, and of Israel, let it be known this day that thou art God in Israel, and that I am thy servant, and that I have done all these things at thy word.

Elijah moved at the proper time for offering that particular evening. Timing is everything when it comes to your success in life. It is critical that you are conscious of the time you have here on earth to fulfill your purpose. You will never become successful until you learn to master your time. If you do not master your time, someone else will master time for you.

Ephesians 5: 15 states, "See then that ye walk circumspectly, not as fools, but as wise, Redeeming the time, because the days are evil. Wherefore be ye not unwise, but understanding what the will of the Lord is." Elijah knew exactly the right time to make his offering to the Lord. Prophetic intelligence will enable you to be in sync with the divine timing of God. In case you may be thinking to yourself, when is the right time for me? The right time is when your preparation collides with opportunity. Now is the acceptable time of the Lord for you to fulfill your destiny.

We mostly think of the prophetic in terms of the future, and this is partially true. Prophetic intelligence empowers you to know your opportunities for today, this very moment. Do you know that many people are suffering pain because they are trapped in some concept of mental time? This happens because they are stuck in the past which gives them a sense of identity, as well as the future, because it holds promises for better circumstances. At the same time, they miss the blessings for today because they are unconscious to now. Think about it.

Most Christian ministers preach messages about a glorious future, and that inspires us. Our fight is to escape the struggles and realities of today. We are usually escapists when it comes to the issue of facing reality.

Perhaps you haven't noticed that your struggle didn't start today, it is the direct result of some chaos that happened in the past. Time is a tool. It is not the sum total of who you are. We identify people with time, such as when we speak of their ages. Never allow time to become your ruler and master. In contrast, take your authority and master time. Time can become a source of pain for you if you become swept away by it.

Natural time is suspended when you are under an open heaven. Joshua 10:12-13 gives us a clear example of how natural time can suspend when you're under and open heaven. Joshua 10:12-13, states, "Then spake Joshua to the Lord in the day when the Lord delivered up the Amorites before the children of Israel, and he said in the sight of Israel, Sun, stand thou still upon Gibeon; and thou, Moon, in the valley of Ajalon. 13And the sun stood still, and the moon stayed, until the people had avenged themselves upon their enemies. Is not this written in the book of Jasher? So the sun stood still in the midst of heaven, and hasted not to go down about a whole day." However, I interpret this Scripture in the metaphorical sense instead of a theological sense. Verse 14 establishes that there has never been a day like that one, neither before nor after it. Ultimately, I will never discount the miracle power of God and say that the sun and moon cannot stand still for you. I believe God will command natural elements to work in your favor to afford you time to complete your assignment.

Personally, I use my prophetic intelligence to maximize my now. There is a golden opportunity waiting for you right now, but you will miss it if you are stuck in the past or struggling for the future. In Matthew the sixth chapter, Jesus admonishes us not to become overly concerned with tomorrow. God declared your ending from the beginning according to Isaiah 43:18-19. He said, "Remember not the former things, nor consider the things of old.

Behold, I am doing a new thing; now it springs forth, do you not perceive it? I will make a way in the wilderness and rivers in the desert." Embrace your today because it is the appropriate time to make your offering to the Lord.

Principle Eight: Eliminate Every False Voice In Your Life.

1 Kings 18:40 And Elijah said unto them, Take the prophets of Baal; let not one of them escape. And they took them: and Elijah brought them down to the brook Kishon, and slew them there.

Once the confrontation ended and Elijah proved that Jehovah was God, it was time for the battle to begin. It was time to annihilate the false prophets of Baal that had been spinning lies to the people that were holding them captive.

You too, must annihilate every false voice that is speaking into your life right now. I am not suggestion that you go and murder someone who is a negative influence in your life. I am saying you must silence all of the wrong information and negative thoughts that are in your life. Let's give notice of Galatians 6:3, which states, "For if a man think himself to be something, when he is nothing, he deceiveth himself." Man deceives himself by thinking the wrong thoughts about his self.

Most people don't realize that they have been a false prophet to themselves. No one has to convince you are a failure when you constantly hold an image of yourself as a failure each day. Likewise, if you hold an image of yourself as successful and prosperous, you will convince yourself to become successful and prosperous.

One of our favorite Scriptures for this type of teaching is Proverbs 23:7, "For as he thinketh in his heart, so is he...." The false prophet within is residing in your mind. This Scripture personifies the Law of Thought, which means you will manifest whatever you think of most. In the Scripture, the heart in the Hebraic is "nephesh," which is translated mind in the English. Therefore, whatever thoughts you focus on most is what you become or attract into your life. If you are not happy with your life right now, visit your thoughts first to find an open door to your unhappiness. Remember this mantra: Thoughts become actions, actions become habits, and habits become lifestyles.

The root of every lifestyle begins with a thought. Thoughts are things and are actual measurable units of energy. Your thoughts are waves of energy that have the ability to penetrate time and space. In addition, your thoughts create physiological changes within your body. Your thoughts, both positive and negative ones, carry energy with them.

These energies attract events and opportunities of like frequency or energy into your life. Let's say for instance, someone has a car accident one day, and to make it better, we will say it wasn't their fault. However, the car crash really was their fault because some thought that they held in their subconscious mind matched the frequency of the car crash. They didn't necessarily sit and think about a car crash all day. The car crash came to them because of some negative thoughts in their life that released energy that attracted the car crash to them.

Never think in terms of what you do not want because your subconscious mind thinks in the literal sense and will embrace every thought your conscious mind produces. You must always think in terms of what you do want. For example, if you want to become thinner and lose weight, your thought should never be I don't want to be fat because your subconscious mind will only hold the image of your being fat. This will result in failed weight loss efforts because of your state of mind. Rather think I want to be thinner and healthy. By doing so, you are giving your subconscious a more positive image to project in your mind.

Here is another example; you get up in the morning thinking I do not want to be late for work today. Out of nowhere, circumstances, events and opportunities to make you late will materialize instantly. This is because your subconscious mind held the image of your being late, and the thought energy attracted situations that would cause you to be late. You have actually been doing this all of your life but have been unconscious of it--until now. The solution to this problem is you must become the watcher of your thoughts.
Take the time out daily and listen to what you thoughts have to say. When you hear your thoughts, do not criticize yourself for negative thoughts. Do this, and you will amaze yourself with some of the negative thoughts that are floating in your mind. Immediately, dismiss the negative thoughts and replace them with positive thoughts. As a result you will become more focused and in control of yourself.

CHAPTER TEN

For the weapons of our warfare are not carnal but mighty in God for pulling down strongholds
2 Corinthians 10:4

MENTAL WARFARE

Your life patterns create opportunities for positive or negative influences to operate in your life. Most people want to rid themselves of the negative influences but rarely do they fight the battle of changing their negative life patterns. Honestly, the path to your success will not be an overnight and easy victory. Daily you must work at your victory. Half of your battle will be won when you begin to elevate yourself to a higher level of consciousness. The battle is not on the physical plane--it is spiritual. Draw your attention to Ephesians 6:12 which states, "For we wrestle not against flesh and blood, but against principalities, against powers, against the rulers of the darkness of this world, against spiritual wickedness in high places." No battle will be effectively fought without knowledge of whom you are fighting. From

Ephesians 6:12, we gather that Satan has a hierarchy of spiritual forces.

First, principalities are the generals and highest ranking forces in Satan's kingdom. Principalities are often referred to as controlling (demonic) spirits that influence specific territories. Second, powers (demons) execute the orders of the principalities. Powers attack against people in the areas of emotion and thought. Third, the rulers of the darkness are demonic spirits that rule over dark systems in the present culture. Finally, spiritual wickednesses are the lesser demons that inhabit the sky or atmosphere. They create evil spiritual climates within a community that affect homes, governments, businesses, schools, and places of worship.

The military forces must have intelligence or information about their opponent. Remember what you learned earlier: the super conscious mind shares prophetic and emotional intelligence with you. When you turn within to hear the intelligence you will be better equipped to fight. The intelligence will reveal to you the negative pattern or influence that is the enemy of your success. These negative patterns and influences, incidentally, open doors into our lives for demonic strongholds.

Also earlier, I defined demonic strongholds as demonically-induced patterns of thought. The mind is the greatest battleground for Satan. Therefore, to rid ourselves of the demonic forces, we engage in spiritual warfare, also known as "astral combat."

We don't have an information shortage, we have a REVELATION shortage.

Spiritual warfare is a conflict between good and evil in the spiritual realm. The greatest spiritual conflict has always been between God and Satan. Understand, this is not a spiritual warfare book, so I am not going to go into the depths of war between God and Satan. All power comes from God, and He has given us the victory over the devil. The devil has no power over your life. Only you can give the devil power or influence in your life. However, my objective in this chapter is to enlighten you about the spiritual warfare that takes place in the mind. There are forces of good and evil which are in constant battle for your mind. Everything that exists is the result of an original thought.

There was a thinker who had a thought that served as a catalyst for the efforts to bring it to materialization. Therefore, we must actively engage in combat against negative influences and patterns that retard our success. The negative forces (demonic spirits) hold people in dismal mental states, disabling them from moving forward in life. Such mental states result in depression, low self-esteem, confusion, fear, frustration, anger, bitterness, and unforgiveness. More than likely, each negative mental state will result in a symptom that adversely effects a person's life such as suicide, alcoholism, drug abuse, racism, sexism, divorce, poverty, and illness to name a few. Trust me, there are many more negative mental conditions that I could name.

God Teaches Us How to Fight Back

The book of Judges sheds light on a group of people left in the Promised Land. Judges 3:1-6, says, "These are the nations the Lord left to test all those Israelites who had not experienced any of the wars in Canaan (he did this only to teach warfare to the descendants of the Israelites who had not had previous battle experience): the five rulers of the Philistines, all the Canaanites, the Sidonians, and the Hivites living in the Lebanon mountains from Mount Baal Hermon to Lebo Hamath. They were left to test the Israelites to see whether they would obey the Lord's commands, which he had given their ancestors through Moses. The Israelites lived among the Canaanites, Hittites, Amorites, Perizzites, Hivites and Jebusites. They took their daughters in marriage and gave their own daughters to their sons, and served their gods. God left these nations in the land so He could teach Israel how to fight a war.

Incidentally, this particular generation had not experienced the former battles of Israel. Young, naïve, and excited to be finally arriving at the Promise Land, God had to prepare them to fight their enemies. Not only did God teach them how to fight, but He also tested their willingness to hear and follow instructions. I want to encourage you not to lose faith in God in your personal battles. The purpose of every spiritual battle is to strengthen you for greater victories. Soldiers must have discipline, mental acumen, and endurance to survive the battle. As the saying goes, "only the strong survive."

The Full Armor of God

God has provided us with special offensive armor and strategies to conquer this spiritual battle. Let's recall 2 Corinthians 10:3-5, which states, "For though we live in the world, we do not wage war as the world does. The weapons we fight with are not the weapons of the world. On the contrary, they have divine power to demolish strongholds. We demolish arguments and every pretension that sets itself up against the knowledge of God, and we take captive every thought to make it obedient to Christ." This spiritual battle can only be fought and won on the spiritual plane. Stop wasting time fighting with people. People are not our enemies. Our enemies are the demonic spirits that influence people. Therefore, we must fight the spirits, not the people.

> I am the way and the truth and the life. No one comes to the Father except through me.
>
> -John 14:6

Ephesians 6:13-17, describes the armor of God,

"Therefore put on the full armor of God, so that when the day of evil comes, you may be able to stand your ground, and after you have done everything, to stand. Stand firm then, with the belt of truth buckled around your waist, with the breastplate of righteousness in place, and with your feet fitted with the readiness that comes from the gospel of peace. In addition to all this, take up the shield of faith, with which you can extinguish all the flaming arrows of the evil one. Take the helmet of salvation and the sword of the Spirit, which is the word of God." Paul uses the armor of ancient Roman soldiers to describe the armor of God.

The Belt of Truth

The Belt of Truth is the first element of the armor of God. The belt held the soldier's armor in place. It also was wide enough to protect the soldier's organs such as the kidney. The soldier's weapons were supported by his belt. Truth provides the support and the protection necessary to stand against the devil. The devil is described in the Bible as the father of lies. Satan uses lies, deception, and counterfeits to persuade us to disbelieve God's truth, which is His word. So many people are bound by delusion and seek fortune, fame, power and pleasure as the most important things in life. Of course, there is nothing wrong with fortune, fame, power, or pleasure but they must be achieved in accordance to God's laws. Therefore, we must walk in God's truth daily to offset this attack. The basis of our warfare and weaponry is God's truth. You cannot walk in truth if you do not know the truth. Jesus Christ is the truth. God's truth can only be discovered by studying His word.

The Breastplate of Righteousness

In any battle, a chest wound is most fatal. The breastplate protected the soldier's heart and lungs. The breastplate of righteousness guards our heart. Scripture teaches us that righteousness and truth are synergistic. Righteousness brings us into right standing with God, which is required to exercise His power. Also, righteousness creates right-thinking in a person's mind. Righteousness protects us from impure motives that disqualify us from operating in God's authority. We cannot stand in our own righteousness against the attacks of Satan.

Acts 19 tells the story of the seven sons of Sceva (a Jewish chief priest) who attempted to cast a demon out of a man. The demon exclaimed that it knew Jesus and Paul but didn't know them. So the demon jumped on the seven men and beat them until they ran naked out of the house of the possessed man. Although the seven sons, used the same method of Paul (the apostle) and the name of Jesus, they couldn't command the demon to leave. What happened? The demon realized they didn't have the authority to command it to leave. Also, there were many self-proclaimed exorcists (person who specializes in removing demons) during that time who emulated Christ's disciples by casting out demons in Jesus' name. These exorcists had no relationship with Jesus Christ but were using His name like a magic phrase such as "hocus-pocus." The righteousness of God is bestowed upon us through our relationship with Jesus Christ. 2 Corinthians 5:21 (Amplified), states, "For our sake He made Christ [virtually] to be sin who knew no sin, so that in and through Him we might become [endued with, viewed as being in, and examples of] the righteousness of God [what we ought to be, approved and acceptable and in right relationship with Him, by His goodness]. Demons are highly intelligent spirit beings and are keenly aware of those who have authority to challenge them.

The Preparation of The Gospel of Peace

Soldiers in ancient Rome walked over rocky terrain. Wearing appropriate footwear was crucial for battle. Paul suggested that we also wear the preparation of the gospel of peace as footwear in spiritual combat. The peace of God is incomprehensible and guards our hearts and minds according to Phillipians13:15. Shalom is the Hebrew translation for peace. It means nothing missing and nothing broken.

God's peace acts as umpire (someone called in to settle disputes) in our minds when we are making decisions. When you are making a decision and you do not feel peace with one or more of the options, give notice to this feeling. God's peace is one of His authorities in our life. God is not the author of confusion. Subsequently, He will never order you to do something you do not have peace with. Colossians 3:15 (Amplified), reads, "And let the peace (soul harmony which comes) from Christ rule (act as umpire continually) in your hearts[deciding and settling with finality all questions that arise in your minds, in that peaceful state] to which as [members of Christ's] one body you were also called [to live]. And be thankful (appreciative), [giving praise to God always]." The peace of God will help you stay in a clear state of consciousness.

The Shield of Faith

The fourth element of the armor of God is the shield of faith. No suit of armor was complete without a shield in ancient warfare. The shield protects the soldier from arrows, swords, and spears. The devil attempts to use his most deadly weapon against us which is doubt. Your faith is the shield against the "fiery darts of Satan" as described in Ephesians 6. Any ounce of doubt is enough to kill your belief in having your desires manifested in your life. Faith is your full confidence that God's words are truth and they will come to pass in your life. Incidentally, faith is one of our greatest defenses against the mental attacks of the devil.

The Helmet of Salvation

The helmet of salvation protects our head, where all thoughts are conceived in our minds. The Father (God) promises that He will keep our minds in perfect peace (Shalom: nothing missing nothing broken) if our minds are focused on Him. Salvation is God's free gift to man restoring him to his spiritual birthright. Through salvation, man regains possession of his God-given attributes. Salvation liberates men from all limitations and directs him (or her) to the path where mind and body may be elevated to a higher spiritual plane of consciousness.

When we lose focus on the truth of God our minds become a playground for Satan. There is a sin called idolatry which means excessive admiration or love shown for somebody or something. The thing or person that is idolized becomes a type of god to the person who admires it. God said in His word to have no other god before Him.

People tend to make material possessions, titles, degrees, positions, power, wealth, and influence, their personal gods. Idolatry was one of the greatest downfalls of Israel (God's chosen people) in the Old Testament. Israel faced many hardships because of their idolatrous ways. Throughout the book of Judges, Israel suffered misfortunes because the Israelites rejected God's truth to worship falsely. Their minds were always captivated by things that displeased God. As soon as they realized what they had done, they would immediately cry to God to save them. Our minds must remain delivered from idolatry in order to live in truth. Likewise, a person who lives in a negative state of mind is unconscious to truth. The unconscious person has no control over what he or she manifests in their life.

The Sword of the Spirit

The sword of the spirit is symbolic of God's word in the Bible. It is the only weapon that we can use to cut down every demonic attack. When we wage war against Satan, only the Word of God can bring him down. "For the word of God is alive and active. Sharper than any double-edged sword, it penetrates even to dividing soul and spirit, joints and marrow; it judges the thoughts and attitudes of the heart." (Hebrews 4:12, NIV) God's word is exactly like a sword with two sharp blades. The term, "double-edge sword," comes from the Greek word distomas which means two mouthed. The idea is that we when we speak in agreement with God's word our words become a double-edged blade against the enemy. A double-edged sword cut the victim going in and coming out. In the book of Revelation, Jesus is described as riding on a horse with a sword protruding from His mouth. We cannot hit the devil or demons with a physical Bible. However, we can cut them by affirming the Word of God in faith. Satan attempts to mix truth with lies to lure us into his traps. In Matthew 4:1-11, we learn how Jesus handled Satan as He attempted to deceive Jesus into disobeying God. Satan's strategy was to use the word of God in a deceitful manner to derail Jesus. However, Jesus countered Satan with the truth of the Scripture each time. Consequently, Satan lost the battle with Jesus and the Bible says that he left for an entire season.

Spiritual Beings Attack the Mind

Demonic spirits' primary battle strategy is to attack the minds of the believer. Although this is a spiritual battle, it is a mental and emotional war as well. God revealed seven enemies that would await Israel in the Promised Land. Even you have spiritual enemies who are waiting to oppose you in the things God has promised you. It is necessary that you fight those enemies until they are defeated. Deuteronomy 7:1-2, states, "When the Lord your God brings you into the land you are entering to possess and drives out before you many nations—the Hittites, Girgashites, Amorites, Canaanites, Perizzites, Hivites and Jebusites, seven nations larger and stronger than you—and when the Lord your God has delivered them over to you and you have defeated them, then you must destroy them totally. Make no treaty with them, and show them no mercy." When Israel arrived at the Promised Land they had a decision to make--either compromise with the other nations or kick them out of the land. Like Israel, you too, have a decision to make. Either compromise with your enemies or annihilate them. After all, the devil is not, nor will he ever be your friend. The devil does not play fair. He only plays for keeps.

In this section, I want to educate you about the nations that represent present day demonic forces in the earth. Please understand that these seven spirits discussed are not the only demonic spirits in the Bible. I am exploring these spirits because I feel we can identify with the struggles of Israel when conquering new levels of success. These spirits attack the minds and the emotions of people locking them into a lower state of consciousness. Our brain is divided into two hemispheres, namely the right and the left. The right side of the brain is associated with our logical reasoning such as truth, law, limitations, established truths, and death. In contrast, the left side of the brain is associated with emotions, creative and intuitive abilities. There is a belief that when the ancient map of Canaan is divided into west and east or left and right, you can actually determine what side of the brain these seven demonic spirits attack an individual. Remember, half of your victory in battle comes from knowing who your enemies are and how they attack.

Hittite Spirit

The name Hittite means "Sons of Terror." This is a subliminal spirit that torments humans through phobias, terror, depression, and deceit. The Hittite spirit brings fear and intimidation to discourage man. People influenced by the Hittite spirit are very prideful and will attack those they perceive as weak. You may observe them to insult, defame, intimidate, and mock those that adhere to godly wisdom. The goal of the Hittite spirit is to wear a person down until their resolve has been broken.

Earlier, I noted that there is a revelation that the geographical locations of the seven Canaanite nations suggest what side of the brain the spiritual entity effects. Maps of ancient Canaan place the Hittite nation on the west side of Canaan symbolizing that this spirit is very comfortable in highly emotional environments.

I want you to know when your emotions are unbridled by law or reason, represented by the brain's right hemisphere, the Hittite spirit may attempt to manifest in your life. A firm grip on your emotional state is vital to combat this demonic presence. Those influenced by the Hittite spirit are usually drawn to things that appeal to their emotions. For example, they may remain in relationships that are unhealthy or prefer to listen to sermons that do not encourage correction in their behavior. God desires for us to live balanced lives. We should not be all emotion without law or vice-versa. Between emotions and law, neither is more important than the other. They are both valuable for us to exist peacefully. Even more, this spirit is chaotic and encourages the disrespect of government and justice. A terrorist by nature, this spirit, is disorderly and hates established authority with a passion.

Girgashite Spirit

Girgashite means "clay dweller." The name further denotes earthliness. Earthly is defined as of, or relating to humankind's material existence as distinct from a spiritual or heavenly one. The Girgashite spirit influences man to believe in what can be seen rather than what is unseen. The Girgashite focus is on that which is tangible and scientifically proven. There is a disregard and disconnect for that which is spiritual or supernatural.

This demonic spirit influences men to reject the truth. We are living in a time where people refuse to accept the Word of God as truth. It is God's truth that makes us free from limitation in our lives. Those affected by the Girgashite spirit tend to be very analytical, and base their decisions on pros and cons that are mentally perceivable. I dare not suggest that it is against God for someone to make decisions based on reason and logic. It becomes an issue when reason, logic, or science overrides our faith for the impossible.

The Bible teaches that, without faith, it is impossible to please God. The definition of faith is found in Hebrews 11:1 (Amplified). It states, "Now faith is the assurance (the confirmation, the title deed) of the things [we] hope for, being the proof of things [we] do not see and the conviction of their reality [faith perceiving as real fact what is not revealed to the senses]." Faith is your personal conviction that you can have, be, or do everything the Word of God says without having physical proof or confirmation. You must not allow the Girgashite spirit to use any natural evidence to negate your faith in God.

It really doesn't matter if you presently have the money, health, and prosperity. What matters is that you believe you will have the money, health, and prosperity. Jesus taught that if we believe the things that we pray for are possible, then, we would have them. I am often asked, "When should people stop believing?" I always respond, "No matter what the circumstances are, we must remain faithful until the very end." Revelation 2:10, offers encouragement, "Do not be afraid of what you are about to suffer. I tell you, the devil will put some of you in prison to test you, and you will suffer persecution for ten days. Be faithful, even to the point of death, and I will give you life as your victor's crown."

The Amorites

The Amorites were mountain dwelling people of some renown. Their name derives from the Hebrew word, amar, which means "to utter, to say." As the meaning of the name suggests, this spirit manifests itself through obsession with earthly fame and glory. People who are affected by this spirit have the tendency to domineer and control people or places. They, like the mountains of the Amorites, impose an enormous and immovable presence. The Amorite spirit has influenced dictators to overthrow and control nations. This spirit looks for seats in high places of authority.

Canaanite Spirit

The name Canaanite means "lowland people" symbolizing to lower consciousness. Ironically, it is the Canaanite spirit that influence addictions and sexual deviance. The Canaanite spirit manipulates the emotions of people in order to hinder the judgment of their mind. For example, when a person is seduced by drug abuse, usually someone has convinced them that the drug is an acceptable method to deal with the pain or stress. Once a person accepts this concept of drugs as being true and acceptable, their judgment is then deactivated. They usually arrive at the point where they no longer hide the addiction and publicly display their emotions. The Canaanite spirit is manifested in a person's lascivious (lustful) behavior. Satan uses the weapon of lust to defeat a person in spiritual combat.

In addition, this spirit influences individuals to become people-pleasers. In order to win against the Canaanite spirit, you must not go against your convictions or change your faith confession to please anyone who disagrees. When I refer to faith confession, I am speaking of what you are claiming by faith in your life such as wealth, healing, or relationship.

Perizzite Spirit:

Situated on the west coast of Canaan, the name Perizzite similar to Hivite it means "village dweller" and "to separate." This nation lived in a village that did not have a protective wall. Thus, the Perizzites lived separated from others in an unprotected village. The devil desires that we live separated from God and without His protection. The Perizzite spirit diminishes the power and creative abilities of those it influences. The Perizzites remained in their own village separated from the other nations. Their separation indicates that they were not concerned with progress. Likewise, the Perizzite spirit's goal is to keep a man in a state of perpetual dwarfism. Instead of growing and flourishing, the victim of the Perizzite spirit is decreasing in spiritual prowess. Ironically, this demonic spirit is closely related to the Hivite spirit except in the fact that it does not influence people to live a life of self-gratification through pleasure. On the contrary, the Perizzite spirit exacts a poverty mentality over those it affects. Moreover, the person is crippled by this spirit, disabling them from making clear mental judgments. As a result, the individual becomes dependent upon others they hold in a higher status.

Hivite Spirit

The Hivites resided on the western side of Canaan. Hivite means "villager" or "dweller in a village or small town." The root word of Hivite, "chavvah" means giver of life. Chavvah is the original Hebrew word for "Eve." When the two words are combined, it implies that Hivite means "dweller in a life-giving village." The destructive spirit captivates people with lower thoughts and emotions of pleasure and power to experience life. Constantly, this demonic power promises its victims life through self-fulfillment. Moreover, the Hivite spirit's main goal is to hinder the mind by filling it with vain imaginations and sensual pleasures. The Hivite spirit is self-willed and self-seeking, only searching pleasure for itself. Families have been destroyed by this demonic power which convinces one mate they cannot live without something they hold more important than their family. In addition, the person influenced by the Hivite spirit may have no desire to create a purposeful life for themselves but are comfortable living off their parent's hard work. Also, the Hivite influenced person is more concerned with enjoying life than having a relationship with Jesus Christ. In our modern times it is very common to hear people say, "This may be wrong, but I have to live my life to make me happy." How alarming is it when a destructive behavior or lifestyle is given more precedence than a life of spiritual peace? God's word says that He has given us all things richly to enjoy, but those things are in accordance with His word. Jesus teaches in Matthew 6:33 that we should seek first the kingdom of God and His righteousness and worldly possessions will come to us.

Jebusite Spirit

The name Jebusite means thresher. A thresher in the Bible is a person who harvests grain out of husk. Threshers used oxen to walk over the husk to tread the grain out of it. The Jebusite spirit seeks to humiliate and demean people in an effort to keep them from growing. Moreover, the Jebusite spirit believes wholeheartedly in the inherent inferiority and seeks to disqualify people from achieving greatness in life. Often, we see the presence of the Jebusite spirit in modern society through racism, sexism, and classicism.

The Blessing Is In Your True Self

While there are times when we wrestle with demonic beings through other people, there are also times when we must battle with ourselves. One biblical account of a struggle with self is found in the story of Jacob wrestling with the angel. This account of Jacob is found in Genesis 32:22-30, "That night Jacob got up and took his two wives, his two female servants and his eleven sons and crossed the ford of the Jabbok. After he had sent them across the stream, he sent over all his possessions. So Jacob was left alone, and a man wrestled with him till daybreak. When the man saw that he could not overpower him, he touched the socket of Jacob's hip so that his hip was wrenched as he wrestled with the man. Then the man said, 'Let me go, for it is daybreak.' But Jacob replied, 'I will not let you go unless you bless me.' The man asked him, 'What is your name?' 'Jacob,' he answered. Then the man said, 'Your name will no longer be Jacob, but Israel, because you have struggled with God and with humans and have overcome.' Jacob said, 'please tell me your name.' But he replied, 'Why do you ask my name?' Then he blessed him there. So Jacob called the place Peniel, saying, 'It is because I saw God face to face, and yet my life was spared.'"

That particular night, Jacob was wrestling with his own personality. He was struggling with his unconscious emotions and having to face his past. Jacob's name means supplanter-trickster or one who is always trying to takes someone else's goods. During most of his life, he lived up to his name, tricking his brother out of his birthright and as well, tricking his father to receive his blessing. He tricked his father in law, Laban out of more than his share of his livestock. What is most interesting about Jacob is that his mother, Rachel, taught him to be conniving as a young man.

Jacob suffered emotionally in fear that his brother would one day return to kill him because of his deceit. Before his encounter with the angel, Jacob received word that his brother Esau was coming to pay him a visit. Jacob immediately sent his wives, children and servants away to safety, as he awaited his brother's arrival. One could only imagine the mental anguish that Jacob must have felt in fear of his brother's anger towards him. The Scripture says that he was left alone and began to wrestle with a man who is later explained to be an angel.

Approaching this interpretation from a metaphysical viewpoint, Jacob wasn't wrestling with an angel but rather his own personality. He was face to face with his past misdeeds and underlying emotions. The return of his brother Esau awakened in him a state of self-awareness. Therefore, he struggled with the psychological force that the text describes as an angel. Jacob struggled to be released from his ego or false self so that he could focus on God within him. Jacob fought all night long which is significant to his state of consciousness.

Many times, day and night in the Bible are symbolism for consciousness and unconsciousness. We mostly deal with our unconscious thoughts or emotions in a dream, which is a state of unconsciousness. This is why the angel had to leave before the morning because the day would bring Jacob into a state of consciousness. Jacob told the angel that he would not release him until he blessed him. Consequently, the benefit of taking control of his desire to please his ego was a blessing. Blessing is defined as the invoking of God's favor, benefit, or mercy upon a person.

Finally, the angel asked Jacob, "What is your name?" He replied, "Jacob," meaning trickster. At last, Jacob is truthful with himself about who he was. For this reason, the angel changed his name from Jacob to Israel meaning one who prevails with God. Biblically, a name change suggests a major transformation in an individual's life. Although, I chose to share Jacob's journey with you, there are others that I could have referred to who experienced a conscious battle that resulted in their name being changed such as Saul to Paul, Abram to Abraham, Sarai to Sarah, and Simon to Peter. Each one of these figures experienced an encounter with themselves that resulted in their name being changed. Biblical names usually represented divine purposes or characteristics of people. The idea here is not for a physical name change but a spiritual identity change. It's time to change your identity from defeat to victory, pain to healed, broken to whole, and poverty to wealth. The list could go on and on. Taking control of your desire to please your ego (false self), will result in a change of identity.

The only way you will finally conquer your personal battle is to conquer yourself. Too often, we escape the reality of who we really are. Above all, it is imperative that you come to a place where you take responsibility for yourself and stop blaming others. Jacob's battle was so fierce that the Bible says the dust rose to the heavens. As a result of his fight he sustained an injury to his hip which left him with a limp. A limp causes a person to move slower on their journey. Whenever we shift in consciousness or any new direction in life, our energies move slower towards that new direction. It's a lengthy process for one to change their habitual paths to follow a new one. Be encouraged. You must be patient and diligent on your path to higher consciousness.

CHAPTER ELEVEN

The thief cometh not, but for to steal, and to kill, and to destroy: I am come that they might have life, and that they might have it more abundantly.
John 10:10

THE CHRIST CONNECTION

Throughout this book we have been on an incredible journey of learning and rising to a higher level of consciousness. I am most certain that at this very moment you are more conscious of the unlimited possibilities that God has awaiting you from the day you were born. Now I want to bring in the key factor that will make every revelation I have shared with you become an immediate reality. Friend, here is the greatest secret I could ever share with you and I have been waiting until the end of this book to reveal it to you. Only seekers of truth will arrive at this moment to finally have the secret revealed. Are you ready? The secret is that there is no longer a secret because the secret was told over 2000 years ago in Jerusalem.

When Jesus Christ was crucified at Calvary, His cross was settled between two thieves. One of the thieves questioned the authority of Jesus, saying if you are who you say you are, then rescue yourself and us, too. However, the other thief said, “Jesus when you come into your kingdom will you remember me?” Jesus replied to that thief saying, "Truly I say to you, today you shall be with Me in Paradise." Traditional Christianity has interpreted this statement from Jesus to mean that the thief would go immediately to heaven after his execution. As a fact of matter, I have no quarrels with the general interpretation. However, I have another interpretation of Christ's statement. I believe Christ was saying at that very moment, the criminal had entered into the realm of consciousness of mind that Christ was in.

This state of consciousness is what the Spirit has impressed me to call kingdom consciousness. Christ says to him, TODAY, or in other words NOW. There is no past or future in the kingdom of God. God’s kingdom is in the present, it's right now. You must perceive that every infinite possibility in the mind of God for you is right now present and not in the future. The criminal became present with Christ in that moment because he became aware of the omnipresence of God. Remember, Eden in the Hebrew means Paradise which is a higher place of consciousness. Paradise for you is not some far distant island hidden away in the ocean. Paradise is discovered when you truly become one with the mind of God or the Super conscious. Jesus declared that the kingdom of God is within you. This is why I believe God did not allow the physical Eden of Adam and Eve to be discoverable. God’s design is for us to turn within to sense or perceive the presence of the kingdom of God within us.

The kingdom of God is where you will access the mind of God and this realm may be entered through Jesus Christ. In John 14:6, Jesus answered, “I am the way and the truth and the life. No one comes to the Father except through me.” In this declaration, Jesus has shared with us a major secret to entering in the realm of the infinite possibilities of His kingdom.

Jesus Christ is the embodiment of the perfect mind, a mind that is consciously unified with divine mind. Jesus Christ asserts that He is the "Way," meaning that He is the example of the manner of conduct, thinking, feeling, and decision making. In speaking of Truth in the Greek translation, Jesus was referring to the quality of personal excellence having pureness of mind without deceitfulness or falsity. Truth is the foundational principle that through the indwelling Christ, man can be consciously aligned with the mind of God. Lastly, Jesus is the Life, lived as a manifestation of being, that was produced as a thought within the mind of God. The spiritual source of life quickens you to the newness of life, mind, body, and spirit. Therefore, we can live the abundant life being quickened.

The only way to conquer your personal battle is to conquer yourself.

It is within God that we live, move and have our being. Jesus Christ is the gateway to kingdom consciousness. Without entrance through Christ, you will not come into the full reality of truth. There is a difference between living spiritual lives, and experiencing the supernatural life. God has dealt a measure of faith to all men so I would dare not say that another spiritual teacher cannot lead you to experience success. I am saying that through Jesus Christ your success will be reached quicker, and more than the material realm, you will live in a spiritual realm that will bring you into oneness of God.

Jesus Christ gave us the greatest example of service and giving. He died a horrific death of crucifixion on Calvary for offenses that He did not commit. His death was not in vain because the Bible said that without the shedding of blood there could be no remission of sin. Not just anyone's blood could pay this debt but only a perfect sacrifice. Jesus Christ was the perfect and ultimate sacrifice because He knew no sin and walked in perfect oneness with God, His father.

Christ was crucified on a hill called Golgotha or also called Calvary outside of the city of Jerusalem. Golgotha in Hebrew means skull, the place of the skull, or shaped like a head. How interesting that Jesus was crucified on a hill that resembles a human skull. I have toured Jerusalem and have seen this hill with my very eyes and it looks exactly like a skull. It is by no accident that Jesus was crucified on skull hill; it symbolizes the intellectual crucifixion that we must experience before we can walk in Kingdom consciousness. You must eliminate every idea, thought pattern, and belief that is blocking your abundance.

Jesus, the intellectual natural man, was crucified so that we could all experience the Christ which is the potential for all men to walk in perfection. His shed blood was not like the red flesh blood that flows through our veins. No, Christ's blood was empowered to cleanse us from an evil conscience to serve our living God. Conscience is defined as an inner feeling or voice viewed as acting as a guide to the rightness or wrongness of one's behavior. The blood of Jesus made atonement for our sins that created a separation between us and the God. We are now able to experience "at-one-ment" with God which allows us to be present with God on Earth. God's presence is neither in the past nor the future but His presence is now and imminent.

> Kingdom consciousness is one's realization of the reality of the kingdom of God

After Christ's crucifixion, He was buried and resurrected in three days. Within three days He rose from the grave in all power. When you experience a crucifixion of a lower consciousness, you will be raised from the grave of an impoverished state. You may not have been financial impoverished, but you may have been spiritual poor. The same Spirit that raised Christ from the dead will raise you from the death grip that you may be in at this moment. Romans 8:11 states, "And if the Spirit of him who raised Jesus from the dead is living in you, he who raised Christ from the dead will also give life to your mortal bodies because of his Spirit who lives in you."

My friend, the greatest moment of success I have ever experienced is when I received Christ as my Lord and Savior. There has been no greater joy in my life than to live in absolute oneness with Christ. Jesus Christ is more than a prophet or way shower, but rather He is the Christ, the anointed one that has come to bring liberty to those who are captive, give sight to those that are blind, and provide prosperity to those who are poor. I invite you to receive Christ into your heart today by praying a simple prayer. Pray this prayer: "Heavenly Father, I come to you in the name of Jesus Christ. Your word said, in Romans 10:9-10, 'That if thou shalt confess with thy mouth the Lord Jesus, and shalt believe in thine heart that God hath raised him from the dead, thou shalt be saved. For with the heart man believeth unto righteousness; and with the mouth confession is made unto salvation.' I do that now. I confess that Jesus is Lord, and I believe in my heart that God raised Him from the dead. Amen!"

If you prayed this prayer, you are now a believer. This is the first step. Go a step further and invite the Holy Spirit to baptize you with His power. Pray "Father, now that I am a believer I ask you to baptize me with the Holy Spirit according to Acts 1:8, 'But ye shall receive power, after that the Holy Ghost is come upon you: and ye shall be witnesses unto me both in Jerusalem, and in all Judaea, and in Samaria, and unto the uttermost part of the earth.' Holy Spirit fill my life now as I praise God. I fully receive you and expect to speak with new tongues as the Holy Spirit gives me the ability as written in Acts 2:4."

Now begin to thank God and praise him for the Holy Spirit filling your life. Speak in the language or syllables that the Holy Spirit is giving to you which is not your natural language. You must use your voice, you are not a puppet and the Holy Spirit will not force you to speak. Now that you are a born-again, Spirit-filled believer, your life will never be the same. I encourage you to find a Bible-teaching church that teaches faith and not religion or poverty and become a part of it. Your new church family will love and encourage you in your faith and you will do the same for them. Please do me one more favor and contact my office to let me know that you have read this book and received Christ as Savior or experienced the Baptism of the Holy Spirit. I want to continue to pray for you in my personal prayer time.

CHAPTER TWELVE

For as the body without the spirit is dead, so faith without works is dead also.

James2:26

CONSCIOUS FITNESS

In conclusion, you must begin to work your conscious muscles each and every day. This new path of enlightenment is a daily journey and it will not happen to you over night. Think about how many years you have practiced this state of lower consciousness as your way of life. It will take a daily conscious effort to shed the old patterns of life that you have been living. Mathew 9:17 instructs us how to deal with new wine. It says, "Neither do people pour new wine into old wineskins. If they do, the skins will burst; the wine will run out and the wineskins will be ruined. No, they pour new wine into new wineskins, and both are preserved." Your operation in kingdom consciousness will never be successful if you do not start forming new habits in life. You are no longer bound by the limitations of intellectualism and reasoning. From this moment on you must decide that you are expecting supernatural results in your life. Expect from this point that your life has taken a radical shift, and you will experience

Kingdom of God results in your life daily. Your world is changing right now as you are reading this book. You do not have to wait five or ten years, a few months or a few days for anything that God has in His mind concerning you. This is your season for sudden supernatural shifts in your world.

According to Scripture, faith without works is dead. Your faith is just like a muscle. If you do not use the muscle, it will lose strength. Trust me; it is going to take faith and courage for you to step into a brand new way of living and thinking. Each moment of faith is followed with an action step. Create your plan for living in a state of higher consciousness, today. Throughout this book I have shared with you steps of action that you can take to begin to see supernatural results in your life. They will only work if you apply them. I am only one coach and of course there are other methods that you may use that work best for you. However, to get you started I have provided some brief exercises that you may use to reprogram your conscious mind.

Techniques for Conscious Living

What is God's agenda for me today exercise

One method that you can use to sharpen your prophetic intelligence is to actually ask questions and write down your answers. Daily, ask the Holy Spirit questions about your day, business or ministry, preferably before you start your day. Journal the answers you hear. The still small voice within or prophetic intelligence as I like to call it will respond to you with an answer but you must open your inner ear to hear. So here are few questions you can use but I encourage you to be creative and develop your own. The purpose is to become more familiar with the voice of the Spirit and how to interact with Him.

Note: Always begin with a period of prayer and worship to invoke the presence of the Holy Spirit.

1. What assignment does the Lord have for me today?
2. Who am I supposed to meet today? (write down details such as name, body description, clothing description)
3. What is my purpose when I meet this person? (encourage them, witness to them, etc)
4. Are there any unexpected issues arising for the business or ministry today?
5. How should this unexpected issue be handled?
6. Who should I eat lunch with today?
7. What should I happen today at lunch?

Make sure you look for these opportunities throughout the day to follow the instructions.

Meditation

The meditation technique is another method you can use to sharpen your prophetic intelligence. Make sure you are in a comfortable position and also where you will not be disturbed. Ask the Holy Spirit for a Scripture and focus on it for a few minutes. As you meditate on the Scripture ask the Lord to share with you every aspect of what this Scripture means to you. This technique will help you maintain focus one thought for a period of time. You may also consider purchasing my Scripture-based guided meditation CD.

I AM Affirmations

You may refer back to the section about the Law of I AM as you use this technique. Develop your personal I AM affirmations that you can recite daily to yourself. Also, create your affirmations from Scriptures to make them more powerful. Here are a few examples:

Affirmations

- I AM precious to God and He cares for me and meets all my needs.- Matthew 6:25-44
- I AM always in the security of God. - Isaiah 41:10
- I AM manifesting my hopes and dreams. - Psalm 119:116
- I AM filled with joy despite yesterday's discouragement. - Isaiah 1:11
- I AM receiving the desires of my heart. - Psalm 37:4
- I AM filled with good things in life. - Psalm 103:1-5
- I AM surrounded by God's unfailing love. - Psalm 23:10
- I AM empowered to create wealth - Deuteronomy 8:18
- I AM money - Proverbs 8:21
- I AM healed - Isaiah 53:5
- I AM maintaining my healing - Nahum 1:9
- I AM creating wealth easily and effortlessly through multiple streams of income. - Isaiah 60:5
- I AM resolving problems with solutions from divine intelligence. - James 1:5
- I AM prospered by everything and everyone. - Deuteronomy 30:9
- I AM appropriately dressed in God's healing. - Jeremiah 30:17

Physical Healing Scriptures

Exodus 23:25
So you shall serve the LORD your God, and He will bless your bread and your water. And I will take sickness away from the midst of you.

Psalm 23:4
Yea, though I walk through the valley of the shadow of death, I will fear no evil; For You are with me; Your rod and Your staff, they comfort me.

Psalm 30:2
O LORD my God, I cried out to You, and You healed me.

Psalm 103:2, 3,5
Bless the LORD, O my soul, And forget not all His benefits: Who forgives all your iniquities, Who heals all your diseases, Who satisfies your mouth with good things, So that your youth is renewed like the eagle's.

Psalm 107:20
He sent His word and healed them, And delivered them from their destructions.

Proverbs 3:7, 8
Do not be wise in your own eyes; fear the LORD and shun evil. This will bring health to your body and nourishment to your bones. (NIV)

Proverbs 4:20-22
My son, give attention to my words; Incline your ear to my sayings. Do not let them depart from your eyes;
Keep them in the midst of your heart; For they are life to those who find them, And health to all their flesh.

Proverbs 16:24
Kind words are like honey–sweet to the soul and healthy for the body. (NLT)

Isaiah 53:5
But He was wounded for our transgressions, He was bruised for our iniquities; The chastisement for our peace was upon Him, And by His stripes we are healed.

Jeremiah 17:14
Heal me, O LORD, and I shall be healed; Save me, and I shall be saved, For You are my praise.

Matthew 9:35
Then Jesus went about all the cities and villages, teaching in their synagogues, preaching the gospel of the kingdom, and healing every sickness and every disease among the people.

Luke 9:1, 2
Then He called His twelve disciples together and gave them power and authority over all demons, and to cure diseases. He sent them to preach the kingdom of God and to heal the sick.

James 5:14-16
Is anyone among you sick? Let him call for the elders of the church, and let them pray over him, anointing him with oil in the name of the Lord. And the prayer of faith will save the sick, and the Lord will raise him up. And if he has committed sins, he will be forgiven. Confess your trespasses to one another, and pray for one another, that you may be healed. The effective, fervent prayer of a righteous man avails much.

III John 2
Beloved, I wish above all things that thou mayest prosper and be in health, even as thy soul prospereth. (KJV)

Financial Prosperity Scriptures

Genesis 8:22
While the earth remains, seedtime and harvest, cold and heat, winter and summer, and day and night shall not cease.

Deuteronomy 8:17-18
Then you say in your heart, "My power and the might of my hand have gained me this wealth." "And you shall remember the LORD your God, for it is He who gives you power to get wealth that He may establish His covenant which He swore to your fathers, as it is this day.

1 Chronicles 29:11-12
Yours, O Lord, is the greatness and the power and the glory and the majesty and the splendor, for everything in heaven and earth is yours. Yours, O Lord, is the kingdom; you are exalted as head over all. Wealth and honor come from you; you are the ruler of all things. In your hands are strength and power to exalt and give strength to all.

Psalm 1:1-3
Blessed is the man that walketh not in the counsel of the ungodly; nor standeth in the way of sinners, nor sitteth in the seat of the scornful. But his delight is in the law of the Lord; and in his law doth he meditate day and night. And he shall be like a tree planted by the rivers of water, that bringeth forth his fruit in his season; his leaf also shall not wither; and whatsoever he doeth shall prosper.

Psalm 23:1 The Lord is my shepherd I shall not want.

Psalm 35:27
Let them shout for joy, and be glad, that favour my righteous cause: yea, let them say continually, Let the Lord be magnified, "*which hath pleasure in the prosperity of his servant.*

Psalm 37:3-5, 11
Trust in the Lord, and do good; so shalt thou dwell in the land, and verily thou shalt be fed. Delight thyself also in the Lord: and he shall give thee the desires of thine heart. Commit thy way unto the Lord; trust also in him; and he shall bring it to pass. But the meek shall inherit the earth; and shall delight themselves in the abundance of peace.

Psalm 37:25-26
I have been young, and now am old; yet have I not seen the righteous forsaken, or his seed begging bread. He is ever merciful, and lendeth; and his seed is blessed.

Psalm 85:12
Yea, the Lord shall give that which is good; and our land shall yield her increase.

Psalm 122:6-7
Pray for the peace of Jerusalem: they shall prosper that love thee. Peace be within thy walls, and prosperity within thy palaces.

Proverbs 3:9, 10
Honor the LORD with your wealth, with the first fruits of all your crops; then your barns will be filled to overflowing, and your vats will brim over with new wine. (NIV)

Proverbs 8:18-21
Riches and honour are with me: yea, durable riches and righteousness. My fruit is better than gold, yea, than fine gold; and my revenue than choice silver. I lead in the way of righteousness, in the midst of the paths of judgment; That I may cause those that love me to inherit substance; and I will fill their treasures.

Proverbs 28:27
He who gives to the poor will not lack, But he who hides his eyes will have many curses.

Proverbs 11:25
The generous soul will be made rich, And he who waters will also be watered himself.

Proverbs 10:27
The blessing of the Lord brings wealth, and he adds no trouble to it.

Proverbs 10:24
What the righteous desire will be granted.

Ecclesiastes 5:19
As for every man to whom God has given riches and wealth, and given him power to eat of it, to receive his heritage and rejoice in his labor—this is the gift of God.

Malachi 3:10, 11
Bring all the tithes into the storehouse, That there may be food in My house, And try Me now in this," Says the LORD of hosts, "If I will not open for you the windows of heaven And pour out for you such blessing that there will not be room enough to receive it. And I will rebuke the devourer for your sakes, So that he will not destroy the fruit of your ground, Nor shall the vine fail to bear fruit for you in the field," Says the LORD of hosts;

Luke 6:38
If you give, you will receive. Your gift will return to you in full measure, pressed down, shaken together to make room for more, and running over. Whatever measure you use in giving–large or small–it will be used to measure what is given back to you. (NLT)

2 Corinthians 9:6-7
But this I say: He who sows sparingly will also reap sparingly, and he who sows bountifully will also reap bountifully. So let each one give as he purposes in his heart, not grudgingly or of necessity; for God loves a cheerful giver.

Philippians 4:19
And my God shall supply all your need according to His riches in glory by Christ Jesus.

Overcoming Fear Scriptures

Deuteronomy 31:6
Be strong and of good courage, do not fear nor be afraid of them; for the LORD your God, He is the One who goes with you. He will not leave you nor forsake you. (NKJV)

Psalm 27:1
The LORD is my light and my salvation; Whom shall I fear? The LORD is the strength of my life; Of whom shall I be afraid? (NKJV)

Isaiah 41:10
So do not fear, for I am with you; do not be dismayed, for I am your God. I will strengthen you and help you; I will uphold you with my righteous right hand. (NIV)

Matthew 10:28
And do not fear those who kill the body but cannot kill the soul. But rather fear Him who is able to destroy both soul and body in hell. (NKJV)

Romans 8:37
Nay, in all these things we are more than conquerors through him that loved us.

Hebrews 13:5-6
For He Himself has said, "I will never leave you nor forsake you." So we may boldly say: "The LORD is my helper; I will not fear. What can man do to me?" (NKJV)

2 Timothy 1:7
For God has not given us a spirit of fear and timidity, but of power, love, and self-discipline. (NLT)

1 John 4:4
Ye are of God, little children, and have overcome them: because greater is he that is in you, than he that is in the world.

1 John 4:18
There is no fear in love. But perfect love drives out fear, because fear has to do with punishment. The one who fears is not made perfect in love. (NIV)

Powerful Biblical Prayers

The Bible is filled with many powerful prayers. The most successful characters in the Bible were men and women of prayer. The following prayers are few of many wonderful biblical prayers that you may pray for yourself and others. As you pray make them personal by including your name or whomever you are praying for.

Our Father Prayer - Matthew 6:9-13 (Pray repeatedly)

Our Father which art in heaven, Hallowed be thy name. 10 Thy kingdom come. Thy will be done in earth, as it is in heaven. 11 Give us this day our daily bread. 12 And forgive us our debts, as we forgive our debtors. 13 And lead us not into temptation, but deliver us from evil: For thine is the kingdom, and the power, and the glory, for ever. Amen.

Paul's Prayer for Spiritual Growth-Ephesians 3:14-21

For this reason I kneel before the Father, from whom his whole family in heaven and on earth derives its name. I pray that out of his glorious riches he may strengthen you with power through his Spirit in your inner being, so that Christ may dwell in your hearts through faith. And I pray that you, being rooted and established in love, may have power, together with all the saints, to grasp how wide and long and high and deep is the love of Christ, and to know this love that surpasses knowledge-that you may be filled to the measure of all the fullness of God. Now to him who is able to do immeasurably more than all we ask or imagine, according to his power that is at work within us, to him be glory in the church and in Christ Jesus throughout all generations, for ever and ever! Amen. (NIV)

King Solomon's Prayer for Wisdom – 1 Kings 3:7-9

Now, O Lord my God, You have made Your servant king instead of my father David, but I *am* a little child; I do not know *how* to go out or come in. And Your servant *is* in the midst of Your people whom You have chosen, a great people, too numerous to be numbered or counted. Therefore give to Your servant an understanding heart to judge Your people, that I may discern between good and evil. For who is able to judge this great people of Yours?"

Hezekiah's Prayer for Healing – Isaiah 38:2-8

Hezekiah turned his face to the wall and prayed to the LORD, "Remember, O LORD, how I have walked before you faithfully and with wholehearted devotion and have done what is good in your eyes." And Hezekiah wept bitterly.